The Librarian's Guide to Writing for Publication

Rachel Singer Gordon

The Scarecrow Press, Inc.
Lanham, Maryland, and Oxford
2004

SCARECROW PRESS, INC.

Published in the United States of America
by Scarecrow Press, Inc.
A wholly owned subsidiary of
The Rowman & Littlefield Publishing Group, Inc.
4501 Forbes Boulevard, Suite 200, Lanham, Maryland 20706
www.scarecrowpress.com

PO Box 317
Oxford
OX2 9RU, UK

British Library Cataloguing in Publication Information Available

Library of Congress Cataloging-in-Publication Data

Gordon, Rachel Singer.
  The librarian's guide to writing for publication / Rachel Singer Gordon.
    p. cm.
  Includes bibliographical references and index.
  ISBN 0-8108-4895-3 (alk. paper)
  1. Library science—Authorship. 2. Library science literature—Publishing. 3.
Academic writing. I. Title.
Z669.7 .G67 2004
808'.06602—dc22

2003014609

Contents

Acknowledgments

Thanks are due to my editor at Scarecrow Press, Sue Easun, who saw the need for an updated publishing guide for librarians. I'd also like to extend my appreciation to the writing librarians who took time from their busy schedules to provide their thoughts and comments in response to an online questionnaire. The editors who agreed to share their perspectives through interviews added useful insight, and I thank them on behalf of both myself and the readers of this book. Lastly, thanks to my beautiful baby boy Jacob, who turned into a regular napper in time to let me finish writing—as well as to my husband Todd, whose support was, as always, invaluable.

Introduction

As librarians, we are accustomed to stretching ourselves too thin, simultaneously juggling multiple responsibilities and activities. It is natural, therefore, that your first response to the thought of writing for publication might be an instinctive reluctance to add another undertaking to your already-full plate of duties.

As librarians, however, we also need to realize that one of the ways we maintain the integrity of our profession is through the creation of a robust body of professional literature. Because we are both professionals and practitioners, we all have "something to say" that can be of use to our colleagues, many of whom are facing similar issues, encountering similar problems, or wondering about similar questions. As Lititz Public Library Director Bonnie Young states: "I think it is our duty to contribute any ideas, thoughts, advice, or experience that will add to [the] professional literature. It is important for the profession to grow and develop. Write about a subject in library work you are passionate about."

While we of course have many more informal methods of communicating with colleagues (including online discussion lists, conversations at conferences, and regular meetings with local interest groups), our professional literature comprises the backbone of librarianship. The literature gives us articles to cite and discuss, a body of work that defines the profession (both to ourselves and to outsiders), and monographs and textbooks to teach aspiring librarians the fundamental issues. It provides a written record by which we can trace the history, issues, and outlook of our profession, and a place to share the fruits of our research with our peers.

Why Write?

Librarians who do choose to contribute to the profession in this way have a number of reasons for writing. These include:

- Having something to say to their peers
- Being required to write for tenure or promotion in their academic institutions
- Wanting to increase the status of their libraries or promote the profession as a whole
- Wishing to share a technique, idea, or program that has proven successful in their libraries with others
- Being required by their administration or a granting body to publicize a program or service
- Wanting to share the results of professional research activities
- Desiring to see their names in print
- Enjoying the writing process itself
- Wanting to give something back to the profession
- Being asked to do so by their administrators or department heads
- Wishing to add to their résumés before applying for a new position

Each of these is a valid reason to write, and each leads to the contribution of different types of work to the diverse and thriving library literature. The single best reason to write, however—one which can and should be combined with any of the above—is to convey your enthusiasm for the library profession to others. At the end of the day, when a hug from a storytime preschooler, a heartfelt thank-you from a student who got an "A" on the paper you helped her research, or a walk through a new computer lab funded by a grant you received reminds you why you got into this profession (and why you stay!), you will glimpse the excitement you need to bottle up and share with your colleagues. The best reason to write for publication is that you are passionate about and engaged by your profession and where it is headed.

Successful and interesting professional communication captures this excitement, whether in a conversation with a colleague, a post to a discussion list, a peer-reviewed research piece, or a feature article in

American Libraries. Writing for a trusted publication just formalizes this communication and gives you both a built-in audience and an automatic boost in credibility in the minds of your readers.

Throughout the book, you will see quotes from some of the ninety-nine published librarians who took the time to contribute their thoughts to a survey on publication in library literature. This survey was posted online from July 2002 until January 2003 at the library careers site Lisjobs.com and advertised on a number of mailing lists, Web logs, and electronic newsletters. Its text is reproduced here as appendix A.

The following chapters will walk you through all aspects of writing for publication in the library environment. Chapter 1 shows how to begin the process of writing for publication, from finding ideas to identifying the advantages of being published. Chapter 2 discusses finding the right outlet for your ideas, while chapter 3 covers the process of contacting editors via query letters and book proposals. Chapters 4-5 give advice on increasing your odds of being published and discuss the actual process of writing and editing your work, and chapter 6 describes the importance of networking to library-related authorship. Chapters 7-9 discuss more specific types of writing, from writing in the academic environment, to becoming involved with related opportunities such as book reviewing and conference reporting, to writing monographs for the library press. Chapter 10, on marketing your work, provides ways to get the word out about your writing and build an audience over time. Chapter 11, on the electronic environment, discusses how the Internet is changing library publishing and how you can use this to your advantage, while chapter 12, on the business of writing, covers contracts, taxes, and other areas you will need to familiarize yourself with. Appendix B includes interviews from editors of a variety of library publications and presses, and the bibliography gives a number of suggestions for further reading.

The book is designed to be read straight through, but you may wish to turn first to individual chapters if you have questions on a particular topic. I hope that the advice and concepts within convince you to dive into writing for library literature, and I look forward to reading all of your contributions! If you have comments or suggestions, please feel free to e-mail me.

Rachel Singer Gordon
Librarian, Franklin Park Public Library
rachel@lisjobs.com

Chapter 1
Getting Started in Library Publication

So, you are convinced that you are ready to take that first step toward writing for publication. As a first-time author, though, you likely have a number of questions and reservations before you are comfortable jumping right into creating your initial article, query, or proposal.

Always keep in mind that you are qualified to write for the profession merely by being part of the profession. Resist the notion that you must be able and willing to construct methodologically strict academic articles, must have universal name recognition, or must put twenty years into your position before being qualified to publish. Since there are so many publishing outlets, and since librarianship encompasses so many specialties and options, the health of our literature depends on the skills of all types of librarians writing at different levels, on different topics, and for different audiences. A diverse literature provides the breadth and uniqueness required for a thriving profession.

Many librarians "start small" by publishing short articles in online newsletters, writing letters to the editor, creating book reviews, or making contributions to a local paper. This allows them to gradually build the confidence and the writing experience needed to tackle larger projects. (For more on related and more informal publishing opportunities, see chapter 8.) Others rework and submit for publication a paper, pathfinder, or bibliography they created in library school. No one requires that your first piece of published writing be a feature article in *Library*

Journal or a peer-reviewed research piece in a Haworth publication; take the time you need to get there.

Also count to your credit any locally published writing you produce, from contributing to your library's newsletter or school's newspaper to writing a grant application. Every bit of writing you create helps you build the experience and the professional recognition you need to go on to do more advanced work. Further, the earlier you start writing and publishing, the earlier your activities will have an impact on your library career—and the more time and opportunity you will have to build your writing expertise and contribute to the literature. One survey respondent stresses that librarians should "begin writing immediately after finishing school. I was told over thirty years ago DO NOT take time to write. It was a huge blow to me and my career."

The more writing you do, the more you will find that the mere act of putting words down on paper (or on the screen!) helps you clarify your own thoughts and provides the opportunity for research into topics of interest—increasing your ability to contribute to the profession, not only through publication, but via your everyday, work-related activities. As Kenneth T. Henson writes: "The combined activities of writing and publishing cause us to escape our routine ways of thinking. Thinking in new ways is energizing. If we are clever, we can direct this energy so that it helps us achieve many of our professional and personal goals."[1] Since as librarians we are all also practitioners, this bond between publishing and practice is especially strong.

Understanding the integration of writing with professional practice is important and a step toward realizing the unique rewards of publication in the library field—which in all honesty is unlikely to be your path to general fame and fortune, although it can be a nice supplement to a librarian's income and a step toward building the name recognition you need for a successful library career.

The publishing survey respondents were overwhelmingly positive about both the professional advantages and surprising ease of being published in the library literature. When asked what advice they would give other aspiring writers, comments included:

- "Do not hesitate to try! It's easier to publish your ideas than you may think."
- "Just do it! There are many opportunities to serve and grow."
- "Figure out what you know more about than many people. You don't have to know everything in the world, or even more than anybody."

- "As a new librarian I was sort of scared about this. I thought that it would be really hard and I wondered if anyone would ever want to know about the things that I questioned. I think that in library literature there is someone out there besides yourself that has the same questions. And because someone out there does, you can find someone who is willing to publish it."
- "Don't underestimate your ability to discover ideas for articles that can get you published—all you need is a good idea with an interesting angle to it. There are ideas everywhere."
- "There are plenty of opportunities out there—it's just a matter of finding the right one(s) for you."
- "Being published is not as difficult as some people may think. In addition to online sources and ALA, there are lots of statewide, regional, or even local avenues for publication. Also, don't think that what you have done professionally is mundane and uninteresting— most people have vast amounts of positive experience that would be wonderful to share via publication, workshop, or other presentation arena."
- "Writing is a joy—while at conferences, on trains, planes, and automobiles, my mind is constantly evaluating ideas for interesting articles. Submitting manuscripts for publication and working with editors is a creative, challenging facet for all librarians to explore."

Most importantly, realize that publication in the library field is an achievable and valuable goal. If you currently lack confidence in your own writing skills, commit yourself both to practicing your writing and absorbing the techniques outlined in this book. You can learn to shore up your skills and develop the confidence you need for success.

Handling Rejection

Realizing the inherent usefulness of the writing process itself will also be helpful during those times when your work does not get published. You should always be willing to submit your work but must also be prepared to deal with the prospect of rejection from the moment you begin to put your writing out there. While rejection is never pleasant, it is an inevitable part of the publication process. Every library author has faced rejection at least once; the important thing is that you do not let rejection (or the mere prospect of rejection) keep you from writing or from submitting your work to publishers.

Keep in mind also that your query or proposal may occasionally be turned down for reasons completely unrelated to the quality of your writing. Perhaps a journal has an article already planned on a similar subject, or perhaps your book idea does not fit in with the scope of a particular press. Maybe your topic is too academic, or not academic enough, for the specific outlet.

Never let the fear of rejection stop you from submitting your work. Your writing may sometimes be rejected, but if you fail to submit it anywhere, it is a sure thing that it will *never* be published. As Trudi Jacobson, coordinator of User Education Programs at the University at Albany, suggests: "Don't let a fear of rejection keep you from writing or from contacting a journal with your idea. I have seen this hamper a number of librarians needlessly."

Also, try to never take a rejection letter personally; you can always try another journal or library press, or you can submit a different query to your first pick. Do realize that editors may be fairly vague about their reasons for rejecting your work; this is largely because they do not wish to get into an argument with potential authors. If they do, however, give reasonable grounds for their rejection, consider incorporating their comments into your work before submitting it to the next publisher on your list. Never write or call an editor to ask him why he rejected your work, and of course never respond in anger. Avoid burning bridges; the library profession is a tightly knit one. Even if you do not intend to submit work to this outlet in the future, you can be certain that news of any unprofessional behavior will spread.

Always have more than one potential outlet in mind for your work. This allows you to move on quickly in case of rejection by the first editor you send it to. It will be useful here to create a list of potential markets for your idea or article, ranked in order of preference. Have the information on each readily available so that if your work is rejected one place, you are ready to submit it to the next entry on your list, which may well have a differing opinion. Gustavus Adolphus College Professor Barbara Fister shares: "The first journal to which I submitted [my piece], one I chose because it reached the audience I thought would be interested, rejected it. I sent it then to *RQ* for their 'information literacy' column edited by Mary Reichel. She accepted it and it actually went on to be named as one of the 'twenty best of the year' by LIRT—sweet revenge for the initial rejection letter."

Most editors, however, do prefer that you refrain from simultaneously submitting your manuscript to multiple publishers. If more than one accepts your work, you then find yourself in the uncomfortable position of rejecting an editor, and most likely torpedoing your chances of writing for that publication in the future.

Those with extra energy and ideas can also consider having more than one query or manuscript circulating at any given time. Even if you receive a rejection for one, you still in this case have hope for the other. (Unless you happen to receive two rejections on the same day, so be willing to play the odds!)

If you are writing for peer-reviewed publications, also realize that reviewers' comments are largely based on their own opinions and convictions. Reviewers can disagree, even at the same journal. Barbara Fister advises: "Don't sweat rejection. I got two blind reviewers' comments once, one very positive, the other outspokenly negative. The negative review was actually helpful in reshaping the piece, which was [then] accepted." Reviewers' or editors' comments can provide the direction you need to rework your writing, make it stronger or more appropriate for a particular outlet, and ultimately get it published.

Determination and persistence will go a long way toward allowing you to ultimately find a publication outlet for your writing. Realize that a rejection letter is not directed at you as a person or as a writer, it merely declines a particular piece of writing for a particular publication at a particular point in time. This should serve as an indication to you that you need either to target your work toward a different journal or that you need to put more effort into shaping it for publication. Chapter 4 gives some ideas on increasing your odds of acceptance.

Finding Ideas

You have likely heard the old advice to "write what you know." Although you should not feel limited to writing only about your immediate experience, this is the best place to start when brainstorming ideas for your work. Since librarians are both professionals and practitioners, much of library literature is based in practical experience. Through your writing, you can share details of how you planned a successful program, conducted a survey, won a referendum battle, received and expended a grant, created a distance-learning portal . . . any professional activity is fair game for publication. You can provide advice to others on job hunting, mentoring, or other career development activities. You can research any area of the profession that you find of interest as a practitioner, in a class, or in your professional reading.

Remember that, when you contribute to the library literature, you are writing for an audience of your peers. Other librarians have an inherent interest in practical articles on issues that arise in everyday library work because many of them will be facing similar problems in their own institutions. Information on how others have struggled, planned, and succeeded is incredibly useful in that context.

Writing about your own professional activities is often the easiest way to get started, giving you built-in topics and providing a wellspring of experience to draw from. As Massachusetts Board of Library Commissioners Consultant Shelley Quezada points out: "Know thy stuff! Who said that? It is the same advice which all writers give other writers—write what you know. If you have good writing skills, and you want to be a 'journalist,' which means you can learn enough about a subject to write a good article, that is also fine. But most librarians will be most effective writing about a great program they have implemented or a service which their library provides." Another survey respondent succinctly notes that: "All of my articles originate in questions that come up as I work."

Be sure when writing these "how we did it" articles, however, that you provide suggestions for how other institutions can duplicate your success. Broaden your scope beyond merely describing how you did it to share ideas on "how *you* can do it," or expand on the implications of your experiences. Try to give your work universal application and appeal.

When describing the impetus for their first published work, most survey respondents describe their initial ideas as growing out of a program they sponsored in their library, a paper they wrote for a class, or a post they contributed to an e-mail discussion list. Ideas naturally evolve from your work or from your research, and merely describing the process of learning from your experiences can make for a surprisingly effective article. Think about what you know, what you have learned on the job, what is important to you professionally, and then share that knowledge with others by writing about it.

Another option is to write on something you would like to know more about or that you have worked on and found of interest in the past. Your background in librarianship means that you can research nearly anything you would like to write about, so do not feel limited to writing strictly from your personal experience if your ideas and interests take you further. If you created a master's thesis or wrote major papers in library school, these can serve as inspiration for future publishable articles. If you have discussed a complex topic in class or among your colleagues that piques your interest, read up on that topic to see if you can identify an article waiting to be written.

Focusing your research around a potential article or book topic can also be one of the most effective ways of learning or of broadening your own horizons. Carol Ebbinghouse writes in a *Searcher* column: "If you really want to learn about something new, commit to write an article on the subject, research the heck out of it, and submit it. . . . This is what I do every other issue—and it keeps me learning—because I would rather share what I learn by writing about it."[2] Sharing what you learn is a natural librarian impulse; give in to it, and begin writing!

Also make a habit of reading widely in both the library field and related areas in order to expand your knowledge base, learn about the current hot topics, get an idea of areas that might be overexposed, and identify subjects for future research and exploration. What issues are currently important to the profession? Do you have ideas or solutions to offer that you have not previously seen in print? What would you like to read about that you have not yet seen written about? Add your perspective to the ongoing conversation.

Cal State San Marcos Library Systems Coordinator Sue Thompson shares: "I read extensively in the literature, both inside and outside the library world. My reading gives me a feel for what ideas are 'hot,' what has been covered and not covered in the literature, and how the process of research and writing are done." Providence College Acquisitions Librarian Norman Desmarais concurs, recommending that potential authors: "Attend conferences and read the professional literature to keep current with the trends and get ideas for hot topics in the profession. When something strikes your interest, research it and write something about it. Often, it helps to keep abreast of literature in different fields as interdisciplinary studies are becoming more important and can contribute substantially to other areas of knowledge."

This means both reading the formal professional literature and keeping up with more informal resources such as Web logs, newsletters, and online discussion lists. Such informal communication lets you know what your peers are thinking and what topics they are passionate about. (See more on electronic communication in chapter 11.) You never know when something you read will strike your interest or will percolate in the back of your mind until you need to refer to it in a future article.

Regular reading in the field can also give you a feel for where gaps may be in the library literature—just waiting for you to fill them! Think about something you would like to see covered in the literature, and then write about it yourself. If you would find a topic interesting, chances are your colleagues would as well. Be sure to watch for publication calendars and announcements of thematic issues in the journals you read; these can show you particular publications' upcoming needs and help trigger article ideas.

The most publishable ideas are, therefore, those that stem from your reading, your research, and your everyday experience. These will be more natural, easier to write about, and more useful than those you sit and literally force yourself to think up for possible publication. Learn to look on all of your professional activities as potential fodder for articles or books. Further, do not feel limited to writing only on one subject or in one general area. Although many librarians certainly build a writing career from specializing in one broad topic, many others are comfortable writing in a number of subject areas. This only makes sense because, as librarians, we are comfortable researching in a number of subject areas—librarianship is the last refuge of the Renaissance person.

If you do, however, intend to build a career from your writing, you may look more closely at the idea of specialization or of finding and filling your own niche in the professional literature. Focusing your energies on one subject area about which you are passionately informed allows everything you write to reinforce everything else you have written. Someone who peruses your latest article or hears you speak at a professional conference may very well go back to see what else you have had to say on the subject and may buy a previous book or books you have written. Editors and conference organizers will come to view you as an expert on a particular topic, leading to writing and speaking invitations to contribute your thoughts on your subject or on related issues. Professional publication goes a long way toward establishing you as an authority on your subject.

Those who intend to make a habit of writing professionally may also wish to begin keeping a file of potential article or book ideas. Jot these down on index cards or in a text file on your PC, making a note whenever inspiration strikes. You may discard a number of these ideas after further research or when revisiting them later, but they can provide fodder when choosing a new direction to focus your work. Writing ideas down will also help you remember them; there is little more frustrating than remembering you had a great topic in mind but finding yourself unable to remember the details.

Above all, try not to force yourself to write on topics or in genres that do not interest you. You may have a publishable idea, but if you lack a personal interest in it, it will be extremely difficult to write on. Your lack of enthusiasm will likely also be apparent to your audience.

Try to pick topics that intrigue you, which will help both you and your readers. Your passion for your topic will translate into the energy you need to produce your manuscript and to keep your writing interesting. Think about the professional issues you have had heated discussions about in your library's staff room, on an e-mail discussion list, or with your relatives, and consider putting your side of the argument down in print.

One survey respondent explains that: "When I've picked a topic that I'm passionate about, it seems that the article writes itself." Another shares: "I enjoy [writing]—and I think that's the key. Find something you enjoy doing in the profession, or enjoy reading about, and concentrate your research on something that interests you. If you just publish because you have to, then you'll never enjoy it." Further, writing about and researching something you are interested in helps lessen the blow if your work fails to find a publisher—you have still added to your own base of knowledge and will be less likely to feel as if you have wasted your time.

Association Assistance

Since writing for publication is a staple activity of our profession (and is even required in many environments for librarians seeking tenure or promotion), you may be able to locate courses or workshops on the subject. These are often offered by the various state and national library associations, and generally take the form of workshops/continuing education sessions presented during meetings and conferences. The Medical Library Association, for example, offered a full-day continuing education course on "Writing For Peer-Reviewed Library Journals" at its 2002 annual meeting, while ALA's Black Caucus offered sessions at its 2002 conference on "Why Don't More Librarians/Archivists Publish?" and "Publishing Opportunities at ALA."

If you have the opportunity to attend an association conference, be sure to visit similar sessions as you embark on your own library publishing career. In-person advice from other librarian/authors at these events can be invaluable and will help give you a clearer picture of what to expect from the publishing process. Attending other conference sessions in your areas of interest can help spark ideas for future article topics. See what speakers are emphasizing and what topics seem popular; this will give you an idea of what subjects may currently be both "hot" and publishable.

Some professional associations offer subgroups specifically devoted to publishing in the field. IFLA has a section on library and information science journals, and ALA's New Members Round Table sponsors an ad hoc committee on supporting new writers. Look for the availability of such subgroups and the amount of other publishing support an association provides as one of your criteria for joining, and take advantage of their activities and support. (For more on association assistance in academic research and peer-reviewed writing, see chapter 7.)

Associations provide financial support for professional research and publication as well. Investigate the research grants made available by associations of which you are a member. The Canadian Library Association, for example, provides $1,000 grants to support original research in the field by CLA members. ALA and its divisions annually sponsor a number of research grants in varying amounts, as well as awards for distinguished published or doctoral research. Any association member is eligible to apply for such a grant; locate opportunities by perusing your associations' Web sites under "awards and scholarships" or "research and publications," or watch for announcement of these grants in your association publication(s).

Also look for grants to underwrite conference attendance, which are available particularly for newer librarians. If you should be awarded such a grant, attend conference programs that support your interest in publication and take time to talk to editors at their booths in the exhibit hall.

Professional Advantages for Authors

Beyond the contribution professional writing makes to the profession, writing for publication conveys a number of personal advantages for career-minded librarians. These include:

- *Promotions or raises.* In an academic environment, raises, promotions, and tenure may be directly tied to your publishing activity. In other environments, any publishing you do both demonstrates your commitment to the profession and helps get the name of your institution "out there." Administrators in any type of library are likely to look favorably on publication in the field. One academic librarian notes that: "Publication is the single most important factor in achieving tenure. It's a bit of a schizophrenic process. The library appointments committee may consider various factors, most specifically related to job performance, but the college committee considers publications to be first and foremost."

- *Name recognition.* Publication gets the attention of your colleagues in other institutions and helps establish you as an expert in a particular field or on a particular subject. It can enhance your professional networking opportunities, as others contact you to comment on your work. You also have an automatic "in" to open conversations by discussing your work with others. Uri Toch, corporate and small business liaison at the Schaumburg Township District Library, comments: "Since I work in a public library, publishing does not directly relate to my career advancement. Nevertheless, publishing does give me a certain 'standing' as it were. It is very nice to be able to go into a library and find materials you have written (whether a book or an article). It also gives a person a certain status to say you have written an article or review." Name recognition never hurts when you are looking for another position or other professional opportunity.

- *Improving your skills as a communicator.* Written communication is important in any library position, and writing for publication helps you hone the skills necessary to craft everything from in-house memos to grant applications to content for your library's Intranet. As Wayne State University Professor Robert P. Holley states: "Writing, even before becoming a professor, is a rewarding experience on its own; but it also makes you think and keeps your viewpoint fresh. Writing skills acquired by publishing also transfer to writing within the library setting where most of us need to write committee reports, articles for various library publications, and lots of memos."

- *Speaking opportunities.* Once you are established as an expert author, you will likely receive invitations to present at conferences, workshops, and other professional venues. This provides another avenue of communication, and as a bonus, you may get paid for your presenting skills (or at least reimbursed for your conference expenses). Norman Desmarais mentions that: "Publication has given me national and international recognition as a scholar and an authority in certain areas. It has led to invitations to speak at conferences, to serve as a consultant, and to write other articles."

- *Improving your own knowledge base.* Writing generally also implies researching and learning to increase your own knowledge of a subject sufficiently to impart that knowledge to others. Danbury

Public Library Web Librarian Janet Foster shares: "Writing/publishing has broadened my scope of the library world. For me it provides a creative way to explore the many aspects of librarianship from technical to customer service, from kids to adults and everything in between."

- *Developing your career.* Researching and writing on topics you wish to know more about can help you develop as a professional—and to explain your professional contributions to your administration and others. Sue Thompson explains: "Aside from being required for tenure, the process of research and writing enables me to take my work to another level. I have been better able to show how my systems work contributes to the library and the library profession."

- *Monetary rewards.* For writers in the library field, realize that these will generally be minimal. (Don't quit that day job!) Still, you do have the opportunity to receive royalty checks for book-length work and honoraria for articles in some professional publications. This is more likely the case at nonacademic journals; peer-reviewed publications generally view being published as sufficient reward in and of itself. One survey respondent shares that "I was paid for a few of my publications, but only an insignificant amount." The minimal financial return on your writing will seem more palatable if you learn to appreciate the intangible rewards of publication, from its impact on your career to seeing your name in print.

- *Networking.* Contributing to the profession through publication is a fantastic way to connect with others. Readers, for example, may contact you to comment on your work, solicit your advice, or invite you to collaborate or contribute to their own efforts. Chicago Library System Automation Coordinator Theresa A. Ross Embrey states: "Professional publication allows you to reach a nonlocal audience of colleagues that you would not normally meet. The exchange of ideas with these individuals has resulted in new insights that I was able to bring back to my current employer."

- *Shoring up your resume.* Publication always adds to your résumé, and publication on library-related subjects helps demonstrate your interest in and knowledge of different aspects of the field. National Library of Australia Librarian Edgar Crook explains: "When I worked in reference, I wrote on other subjects. . . . When I came to change jobs, even though I had not worked in a subject area I was going for, I could show by my publication record that I had been thinking and writing in that area, if not actually working there."

- *Keeping you connected to the profession.* Even if you are writing about programs you have implemented in your own institution, the mere process of tailoring this writing to a wider audience forces you to think about issues in terms of their professional impact. Bloomington Public Library Public Services Librarian Rochelle Hartman says that: "What publication has done, though, has gotten my head out of my immediate surroundings, and prompted me to look at larger issues of librarianship. I've met and heard from several people outside of my library because of my publications. Broadening my scope of acquaintances and knowledge of library issues has been invaluable. I think it makes me a better librarian. It certainly makes me a happier librarian."

Overall, writing for professional publication provides an avenue by which you can become more involved in the profession and help advance your own library career. Writing is also one activity that is equally open to all librarians, no matter the size or type of their library or the amount of professional support they receive from their institutions. It is one of the best ways to remain connected to other librarians and to clarify your own ideas about professional issues, helping you, both formally and informally, to move forward in the library profession.

Notes

1.   Kenneth T. Henson, *Writing for Professional Publication: Keys to Academic and Business Success* (Needham Heights, Mass.: Allyn & Bacon, 1999): 21.
2.   Carol Ebbinghouse, "Would You Hire You?: Continuing Education for the Information Professional," *Searcher* 10, no. 7 (July/August 2002): 114-15.

Chapter 2
Submitting Your Work

After you have settled on an article or book idea, your next step involves deciding on the best outlet (or outlets) for your work. There is no one right answer to this dilemma, as your choice depends on factors as varied as your topic, your intended audience, the length of your proposed work, whether you need peer-reviewed publication for tenure or promotion, and your tone (academic, practical, or personal). All types of library presses and journals, large and small, academic and general, online and offline, are currently flourishing. This is good news in that a multiplicity of outlets means a greater need for content, but it also means that you will need to be prepared to devote some time to deciding on an appropriate place to submit your article or monograph idea.

The multiplicity of library-related publishing outlets is welcome news for aspiring authors in that even if your first attempt is rejected, it may yet be welcomed at another publishing house or journal. Have a backup choice or two in mind, remembering that it is entirely possible for your work to be rejected by a particular outlet due to factors other than merit. If you feel strongly about the value of your proposed topic, rework it to fit another publisher's guidelines and send it right back out. Find some guidelines for choosing appropriate outlets in table 2.1.

Start your quest for appropriate publishers by creating a thorough mental picture of the group of readers to whom your work will be of the most interest. When choosing the appropriate home for your own writing, you must first determine your natural audience—based on the

Table 2.1. Questions to Ask Yourself before Choosing an Article Publication Outlet

1. Do I need to publish in a peer-reviewed outlet in order to be considered for tenure or promotion in my institution?

2. Is the relative prestige of a journal important to my tenure or promotion prospects?

3. Is my topic targeted toward a specific audience (serials librarians, new librarians, etc.)?

4. Is it important to me to be monetarily compensated for my writing?

5. How long an article does my topic lend itself to being?

6. Is it important to me that I maintain the copyright of and control over my work?

7. Is my topic localized, or will it be of interest to librarians nation- or worldwide?

8. Is my topic more academic or more practical in nature?

9. Is it important that my research be published in a timely manner, or is my topic evergreen?

proposed topic, length, approach, and tone of your work. This allows you to identify potential publishers by examining the typical audiences for a variety of library publications or presses. Always have your audience in mind, both when proposing your idea and during the actual writing process.

In order to write for this target audience, you will want to select your ideal publication and read its guidelines prior to actually beginning the writing process. You do not want to write an article and then learn that it is a good 2,000 words over your target journal's maximum length, or that they require a nonacademic tone, but your work is instead a heavily footnoted report on a research study you've conducted. While you may need to do some rewriting if your first pick turns you down, avoid having to do so before you initially submit your article or query.

If you have a number of articles or queries "out there" at any one point, you may also wish to make a habit of tracking your submissions. Simply keep a running file in MS Word or in your editor of choice that lists your queries, the date you sent them, who they were sent to, date of response, and status (acceptance or rejection) for each. Leave room here to track each manuscript through multiple tries so that you can easily see where you have previously submitted each.

Also keep in mind that many publishers frown on simultaneous submissions. While this may seem a good way to maximize your odds of success by getting your query or manuscript in front of a number of editors at a time, if more than one says yes, then you are in the uncomfortable position of having to turn editors down. You are also most probably making them less likely to consider your work in the future, due to their wasted time and effort. In academic publishing, simultaneous submission also runs the risk of wasting the time of busy reviewers.

Familiarizing Yourself with Journals

Newer writers will likely begin their quest to be published with library journals and newsletters, rather than proposing a monograph idea right off the bat. Many librarians build an entire publishing career by writing articles without ever having the need or inclination to publish anything longer. Journal articles form the backbone of our professional literature, which requires a consistent supply of new authors and new ideas.

There is a huge number of article publishing outlets available to the aspiring librarian author, falling into several major categories. General outlets, such as *Library Journal* and *American Libraries*, publish nonacademic articles and news stories on a variety of topics. Subject-specific outlets, such as *VOYA* and *Computers in Libraries*, publish general articles focused on a particular topic or for a specific audience. Peer-reviewed, scholarly publications, such as *The Journal of Academic Librarianship* and *LIBRES*, provide outlets for those wishing or needing to publish academic research articles in the field. Newsletters and 'zines, both on- and offline, give librarians the opportunity to make shorter and more informal contributions to the literature.

In order to submit the appropriate query or manuscript to the appropriate journal, you will need to familiarize yourself with the types of articles published by a variety of outlets. Journal editors generally fail to appreciate writers who display a lack of familiarity with their publication or with its contributor guidelines. Never submit a query or article to a journal without knowing the journal's audience and style; your best hope in this case is to receive a politely worded rejection stating that your contribution "is not right for our publication," and you will only waste your time and that of the editor.

The best way to become familiar with a journal is to read it regularly, and you will want to make it a habit to read (or, at the very least, skim!) as widely as you can in your field. While reading, make note of the length, tone, style, and topic of articles in various journals; this will enable you to match your queries to the appropriate outlet. Before submitting, be sure to read the most recent issues to find out whether a journal's style, audience, content, or editor have changed. See whether it includes a publication calendar or instructions to authors in each issue and consult these guidelines before choosing any journal as the right publication for your work. Read each issue's editorial, which will often contain comments on what the editor has found useful in the articles in that issue and ideas he/she would like to see explored in the future.

Also take advantage of the free samples that many publishers offer. Write and ask for sample copies of journals you find useful; in many cases you can order a sample copy on the journal's Web site. Some publishers offer limited-time full-text access online to selected journals. Emerald, for example, provides access to a "journal of the week" on their Web site and allows all visitors to browse through current and past issues of that publication free of charge during that time at http://www.emeraldinsight.com. They also provide a free thirty-day trial to abstracts of their entire database for first-time visitors. Take advantage of such offers when you are ready to spend significant time familiarizing yourself with a publisher's offerings.

Take some time as well to browse through any staff journals to which your institution currently subscribes. Be sure that you are on the internal distribution list for each; although it may take some time for the most current copy to wend its way to you, at least you will be able to get a feel for each publication's content and tone. Also ask colleagues and mentors in your institution about the journals they find particularly valuable. While reading these journals, pay special attention to articles that are similar in subject or approach to topics you may wish to write on. Spend some time thinking about how your treatment will differ from or complement the existing literature.

If you work in an academic institution, also consult relevant journals the library maintains in its collection—set aside some time each week to browse recent issues. You may need to devote after-hours time to this, but your research and reading will pay off as you develop your writing career. Make photocopies of or notes about articles that are relevant to your own areas of interest so that you can use these ideas as background for your writing, being sure to give appropriate credit to the authors on whose work you draw.

Most libraries, however, subscribe to a relatively limited number of journals. You will need to expand your approach in order to identify other appropriate outlets for your work. Begin by exploring the most relevant professional associations for your field of librarianship and your research/writing interests. In addition to the other professional advantages that accrue from association membership, note that many associations and organizational subgroups publish journals or newsletters, which are automatically sent to all members as part of their return for their annual membership fee. This helps make membership a wise investment, as these publications provide you with additional topical outlets and background for your own writing.

Your next step will be to widen your scope even further by identifying any relevant journals to which your institution does not subscribe, but which are available, in full or in part, online. (See chapter 11 for more on reading and researching online.) An Internet search on your subject may link back to such journals, or use the resources in table 2.2 to locate publications' Web sites. Take a trip to your local library school's library, browse print journals, and then search on the names of the most promising titles to identify their online presence. Use *Library Literature* or *LISA* to locate articles of interest, then search for the journals' web sites. Follow the links from Web logs or online newsletters to interesting articles, then back up to the journal's home page and bookmark it for later reference.

Also watch for "calls for contributors" on e-mail lists and Web logs, which will generally link back to a publication's Web site and allow you to peruse fuller guidelines, publication calendars, and sample articles online. (Answering such a call for contributors can be a sure way to improve your odds of acceptance, as it is a pretty good indication that the publication is currently short on articles!)

One of the best ways of identifying appropriate journals to which you can submit your work is by merely beginning the research or background reading process for your article. Keep track of the publications where the other researchers or writers whose work you draw on are most often published. Take advantage of any full-text online periodical databases your institution subscribes to; often these include the ability to browse through other articles in the same journal issue, once you have located a single piece of interest. Use this "browse" feature to

Table 2.2. Selected Resources for Locating Library Journals

- Bahr, Alice, ed. *InPrint: Publishing Opportunities For College Librarians*. Chicago: ACRL, 2001. http://acrl.telusys.net/epubs/inprint.html

- Electronic Journal Miner: http://ejournal.coalliance.org

- *Fulltext Sources Online*. Medford, N.J.: Information Today, semi-annual. Weekly updates (subscription-only) available online. http://www.fso-online.com

- *Gale Directory of Publications and Broadcast Media*. Farmington Hills, Mich.: Gale, annual.

- Nesbeitt, Sarah L., and Rachel Singer Gordon. "Appendix B: English-Language Library-Related Publishing Outlets with an Online Presence." *The Information Professional's Guide to Career Development Online*. Medford, N.J.: Information Today, 2002: 345-64. http://www.lisjobs. com/careedev/appendix_b.htm

- PubList.com: http://www.publist.com

---

familiarize yourself with a journal's tone and style by reading entire issues via a database.

You can also consult a number of on- and offline guides to journals in the field. Table 2.2 lists some places to begin your search for appropriate publications.

Once you have become familiar with a number of journals in the field, this knowledge will help you put together an appropriate list of publications to which you can consider submitting your work. Whenever you submit an article or query, use your list and your knowledge of such publications to identify the best few outlets for a given article. Starting with the journal in which you would most like to see your article published, begin submitting to each outlet in order. If an article or query is rejected by your top pick, send it out immediately to the next journal on your list—incorporating any necessary changes to make it appropriate for that publication. If editors include comments on your work with their rejections, take these into account before resubmitting elsewhere. Welcome any chance to incorporate another perspective.

You should also consider the relative prestige of a publication outlet when deciding where to submit your work, especially if you are in an academic environment. Publication in journals that are often read and often cited, or that are perceived as relatively more difficult to break into, will be looked on more favorably than publication in less-prestigious journals. Consult online citation indexes or sources such as ISI's Sci-Bites (http://in-cites.com/research/2002/october_28_2002-1.html) to help get an indication of the relative impact of various journals. Also make a habit of browsing the notes and bibliographies of articles and books on subjects similar to your own to see what publications they most often cite; these are publications you should look at being published in yourself.

Prestigious and well-known journals have correspondingly high rejection rates, however, mainly because they receive the largest number of submissions. If you are just starting out in library publication, you may wish first to target smaller, lesser-known, and more accessible journals to build up your writing skills and reputation before submitting to one of the "big names."

Familiarizing Yourself with Publishing Houses

Library publishing houses, from ALA Editions to Information Today to Scarecrow Press, provide homes for longer, book-length works. Like professional journals, these publishing houses differ greatly in their approach and in the types of manuscripts they publish. Some are appropriate outlets for book-length scholarly titles, while some specialize in practical, "how-to" books for the library practitioner. Some focus on subfields of the profession, such as technology or reference materials, and some are larger and more formal than others.

Continue your practice of reading widely in the literature by familiarizing yourself with the material published by the major library presses. When reading or consulting titles in the field, always make a note of the publisher—over time you will get a feel for the specialties of each house. If you run across a title which is similar in content or tone to your proposed monograph, see who published it. Read the acknowledgments in the books that are most useful to you. If authors thank their editors by name, this is usually a good sign. Get recommendations from your colleagues and other authors; see what their experiences have been with different publishing houses.

Some of the resources in table 2.2 will also be useful in locating library presses. Peruse their Web sites, and, if author guidelines are not available online, write or phone to request a copy. Look to see if the press on its Web site describes the types of manuscripts or topics it is actively seeking. Get on mailing lists to receive current copies of publishers' catalogs, which are a great way to familiarize yourself with a publishing house and to keep track of new developments in the field. Read reviews of professional literature in the major journals, such as *Booklist*, *American Libraries*, and *Library Journal*, as well as in journals devoted to covering your particular subfield of librarianship. You can then interlibrary loan or purchase your own copies of the most relevant new works.

There are a number of considerations when choosing the most appropriate library press for your own work. These primarily include:

- Large or small publishing house? Larger publishers have the advantage of having a larger amount of resources that can be devoted to publicizing and promoting your work. Publishing with a larger, well-known house also gives your book a certain amount of prestige. Smaller presses, on the other hand, may be able to devote more time and personal attention to your title. They can also be more flexible and more willing to take risks on books that are likely to have a smaller print run or make less money for the house.
- Academic or popular press? As always, this depends on the tone and focus of your title and on your own needs. If you are in an academic institution and publishing with a scholarly press would improve your chances at tenure or promotion, see if your topic could be appropriate for such a publisher.
- Library-only or general publisher? Some publishing houses, such as ALA Editions and Neal-Schuman, specialize solely in titles in the library field. Others, such as Scarecrow Press, focus on a number of fields. Think about how important it is to you that your editor be a librarian or that your press focuses entirely on library science.

Chapter 9 further discusses the process of choosing a library publisher, and table 9.1 on page 100 lists contact information for some of the major presses.

Finding and Following Guidelines

When submitting your ideas to journals, always find (or request), read, and strictly follow a publication's current guidelines regarding queries and manuscript preparation. This is important for three reasons. First, by writing and querying according to guidelines, you create less work for your editor—always a plus! Secondly, ignoring guidelines betrays an unfamiliarity with both the guidelines and the publication, and editors are not keen on authors who do not bother to read the journal they spend so much time putting together. Lastly, following guidelines allows you to submit work that is appropriate for a particular publication, allowing them to consider your article on its content and merits rather than rejecting it automatically on the basis of an inappropriate topic, style, or format.

This also holds true for journals which follow a publication calendar or sponsor thematic issues. Query only about article ideas that fit their upcoming topics. A journal will be unable to use your work, however well-written, if it does not fit its upcoming themes, and you will wish to show that you have followed their explicitly stated wishes for article topics.

Most journals today have Web sites where they post their contributor guidelines and other useful information for potential authors. (These may be titled "Notes to Contributors," "Guidelines," "Instructions to Authors," or any variation on the theme.) Be willing to spend some time digging through various sites to locate guidelines, which are not always linked prominently from a journal's home page. Consulting journals' sites reduces the need to request and wait for guidelines to be sent via postal mail, helping to speed up the publication process.

Table 2.3 provides an example of contributor guidelines for an online newsletter. Note that, while brief, these guidelines describe the types of articles needed for the newsletter, provide URLs for further information on issue themes and archived articles, indicate the length and format of ideal articles, and provide an e-mail address for queries. You can tell at a glance whether your article idea is appropriate for this publication and how to submit your ideas.

Contributor guidelines will sometimes outline the format and style required for completed manuscripts as well as the preferred method of querying; in other cases you will be provided with separate manuscript guidelines after your query is accepted.

Table 2.3. Sample Contributor Guidelines, *Info Career Trends*

Information for Contributors

If you are interested in contributing an article, book review, or Web review to *Info Career Trends*, first take a look at the upcoming themes (http://www.lisjobs.com/newsletter/theme.htm) to see if your idea fits into one of these topics. If you have an idea for a theme not listed here, please e-mail editor@lisjobs.com to make your suggestion. *Info Career Trends* focuses on issues relevant to practicing librarians and is not interested in heavily theoretical or academic treatments. Consider how your topic will be of use to working information professionals.

Current needs are:

- Practical, "how-to" articles—suggestions for how librarians can contribute to their own professional development or how managers can help develop their employees.
- First-person articles discussing how the author has taken action to develop his or her career—providing models others in similar situations can follow.
- Book/Web site reviews—resources to help librarians grow as professionals.

Before sending an entire manuscript, please query via e-mail to editor@lisjobs.com. In your query, briefly describe your idea for an article, how you intend to approach the subject, and why you're a good person to write about it.

Completed manuscripts should be 800-1000 words in length. Reviews should be under 150 words. Since *Info Career Trends* is distributed by e-mail, longer articles are not currently acceptable. The newsletter is nonacademic—footnotes are rarely acceptable, and style is somewhat informal. Before submitting an article, be sure to consult previous issues, available online in the *Info Career Trends* archive (http://www.lisjobs.com/newsletter/archives.htm), to help give you a feel for the newsletter's style and needs. Article deadlines are generally the first Friday of the month before the relevant issue.

Submit your manuscript via e-mail, preferably in plain text (as an attachment or within the body of the message). Submissions are also accepted in Microsoft Word (.doc) format, but note that all formatting will be lost due to the means of distribution of this newsletter. Please single space after periods and other punctuation.

Info Career Trends asks only for one-time electronic rights (e-mail and Web, including permission to archive your article online), and the copyright for your article will remain with you. The newsletter does not pay contributors but will include short biographical information and a link to your Web page or other online resource for librarians.

(From: http://www.lisjobs.com/newsletter/theme.htm#contrib.)

   Follow the same process of finding and following guidelines when submitting your book proposal to publishing houses. Most will have guidelines readily available for prospective authors (see table 3.2 for an example), and following those guidelines will help the publisher make an informed decision on your proposal.
   Journals maintain guidelines in order to encourage the submission of manuscripts and article ideas that are appropriate in format, tone, subject, and style. An article or query that meets one publication's guidelines and needs is unlikely, without some revision, to match what is wanted by another, and editors' most common reason for rejecting a manuscript is that it fails to meet the guidelines and stated objectives of a journal. In an informal poll on NMRTWriter in March 2003, one of editor's most common pet peeves was writers' refusal or inability to follow guidelines. Following guidelines is the simplest way to get your foot in the door and can go a long way toward increasing your odds of acceptance.

Chapter 3
Queries and Proposals

There are a number of ways to approach editors with your ideas. Each editor has his/her own preference, which should be spelled out in a publication's contributor guidelines or in a publishing house's instructions to authors. Some publications will evaluate only completed manuscripts. Before taking the time to view a finished piece, however, many library journals and monograph publishers will wish to see a query letter (which briefly outlines your proposed work) or a book proposal (which more thoroughly explains your project). Your mastery of the fine art of querying and proposing will be a giant step toward finding a home in the library literature for your writing.

A well-crafted query letter shares much in common with an effective cover letter that you might use when applying for a new position. Each enumerates your qualifications, remaining professional while still allowing your personality to shine through. Each describes the benefits your selection will bring, here, outlining the article or book you intend to write for the publisher and showing how it matches their needs and readership. And, like a cover letter, a query letter can make or break you when it comes to doing work for a particular library publication or publishing house.

The basic purpose of a query letter is to introduce yourself and your idea to publishers, allowing them to determine if your proposed article is appropriate for their publication or book is appropriate for their press—and if you are the right person to write it. In one brief letter, you must describe what you intend to write about, explain why you think your topic is appropriate for this publishing outlet, and demonstrate your qualifications for writing on the subject. Again, just as with a cover letter, limit your query letter to one page. Editors are busy people and will most likely assume that rambling letters signify similar problems with your proposed work. Use your query to demonstrate both your writing ability and your knowledge of your subject.

You will often wish to query a journal prior to actually writing an article. The exception here is in academic publishing, as peer-reviewed journals that publish research papers generally prefer to see full manuscripts or article abstracts rather than a simple query letter—it is difficult to assess the validity of your research from a query. Journal guidelines will spell out the preferences of a particular publication. Many editors of general library publications, however, will wish to see a initial query rather than a finished work. You want to avoid wasting your time and their time by creating an entire piece of work that turns out to be inappropriate for their journal, or by writing a piece on a topic which is already slated to appear in a future issue.

Publishers who are kind enough to specify in their guidelines the elements they wish to see in a query greatly simplify this process for their authors. While most publishing houses will not address queries in their guidelines, they will instead be very specific as to their book proposal requirements. You may, in this case, either query first to see if the publisher is interested in seeing your book proposal, or simply send in a complete proposal that meets that publisher's guidelines.

If you are querying someplace that does make the effort to outline specifics, be sure to address all of their requirements; they are included for a reason. Some journals are unfortunately not as accommodating, leaving you on your own when it comes to structuring an effective query letter. There are, however, several elements common to most queries that will help potential publishers ascertain whether your topic and your writing abilities are appropriate for their publication. If guidelines are not provided, including these elements in your letter can help increase your odds of being published.

The specific elements required in your book proposal will also vary according to the guidelines of each library press, although each set of guidelines will generally cover similar ground. Having an idea for a manuscript is simply the first step in a lengthy process, and your next move will be to use the proposal you create to convince a publishing house of the merits and salability of your work. Although it may seem that a great deal of effort is involved in composing an effective proposal, each of these elements is necessary in helping a library press decide whether your book will be right for them.

The work you do on a proposal now will also provide background material for you to use later, while you are composing and marketing your manuscript. As Susan Rabiner and Alfred Fortunato point out: "Editors know what makes a good book. The questions an editor wants answered in a proposal are the same questions you must address to write a worthwhile book."[1] Thus, a proposal serves the dual purpose of selling your idea to a publisher and of clarifying your own thoughts, preparing you to later write the actual book.

Note also that there are almost no circumstances under which you will wish to write your entire book before writing and submitting a proposal. If you compose an entire manuscript, and no publisher accepts it, you will have wasted a great deal of time and effort. If you compose an entire manuscript, and a publisher does accept your idea but wants a change in its tone, focus, or the topics included, you will need to do a great deal of rewriting. Further, most publishers will not take the time to evaluate an entire manuscript for publication; they want to see a proposal first. Never submit an entire unsolicited manuscript, as editors do not have time to read whole titles on the off chance that their house may be interested. While fiction authors are often instructed to complete their manuscript before shopping for a publisher, the opposite is true for nonfiction and professional writing.

Query Letters

Keep in mind that your query letter's main purpose is to sell your idea—and to sell you!—to a potential publisher. Every element in your letter, therefore, needs to work toward that goal. A common pet peeve among editors is receiving query letters that tell them little or nothing about the proposed work or about the author. As an editor of an online newsletter, for example, I often receive e-mailed queries that read something like: "I'd like to write for the next issue, so what's the deadline?" I have never accepted such a query, and it is difficult to imagine an editor who would. This query at the very least needed to explain: *What* do you want to write for the next issue? *Why* should you be the person to write it? *How* do you intend to present your work? Avoid writing overly broad, brief, or unclear queries. Make sure that your topic is clear in your own mind before querying an editor.

Another common mistake beginning writers make in their queries is to confuse enthusiasm with a lack of professionalism. (I once received a memorable query that began: "Yo, Miz R!") While varying levels of formality are appropriate, given the type of publication and your previous relationship with an editor, remember that you are here trying to establish or maintain a professional connection. Check your spelling, address your query to the appropriate editor, and remember that your query is your chance to make a professional first impression on your editor. Since first impressions are often lasting impressions, take this opportunity to impress!

Elements of a Typical Query

Begin your query letter with an introduction that will pique your editor's interest in your topic. Think of what makes your proposed article (or monograph) unique and interesting, and summarize this in a short yet compelling introductory paragraph. You wish to infect your editor right off the bat with the same enthusiasm you feel for your topic.

Following your introductory paragraph, concisely describe the article or book you intend to write. Outline the information that will be included, the proposed length of your work, and any conclusions that arise out of your research. Do not give a simple sentence stating your topic; use this paragraph to explain exactly what you intend to write about, what angle you will take, and what conclusion you will draw.

For journal articles, then describe how your article fits the publication's needs. Is there a particular section for which your work would be appropriate? Is there a forthcoming thematic issue for which you are proposing a topic? Customize your query to a particular journal; do not send the same generic query out with all of your article ideas. Show that you are familiar with the publication and that your article applies to their audience.

Now, explain why you are the person to write this article or book. Do you have particular experience in the area? Have you spent time researching a subject? Have you compiled survey responses or statistics? Have you written articles on similar subjects? Does your educational or work experience bolster your claim to expertise on your topic? Show that you are qualified to write this particular piece for this particular journal. Here, you can also mention any "clips" (copies of previous publications) you are including or provide citations to your writing. If you have published a number of articles, include those that are

Table 3.1. Query Letter Example

July 21, 1999

PO Box 6931
Villa Park, IL 60181

Tarshel Beards
Acquisitions Editor, ALA Editions
50 E. Huron St.
Chicago, IL 60611

Dear Ms. Beards:

With your background in both electronic resources and user instruction, you are familiar with the necessity for libraries to educate the public on the use of electronic library resources, particularly the Internet. Unfortunately, a large number of the 73 percent of public libraries offering Internet access to their patrons lack either the time or resources to implement effective user training programs.

Most available publications aim at teaching librarians themselves to become more effective Internet researchers, rather than serving as a practical guide for them as they attempt to design and teach Internet classes to patrons.

I propose a book titled *Teaching the Internet in Libraries.* Such a title would be useful, not only to public librarians, but in school libraries and academic libraries facing similar user-training challenges. The book would find an additional market as a resource for LIS classes on subjects such as the Internet in libraries and technology training.

Please find enclosed a project proposal and a SASE for your convenience, as well as a résumé and several clips. My background as a reference librarian and experience in teaching and preparing materials for the public enables me to present ideas both clearly and succinctly, and my experience designing and teaching public Internet classes, preparing printed material, and designing library Web pages for class use has given me insight into the necessary elements in a successful training program.

If you are interested in this project, I would be delighted to send a more detailed proposal or to discuss it with you further. Thank you for your consideration, and I look forward to hearing from you soon.

Sincerely,
Rachel Singer Gordon

Phone: 630-555-5555
E-mail: rachel@lisjobs.com

most pertinent to this query; if you have seldom been published in the past, include any available clips.

Your concluding paragraph should wrap up the query and clinch your argument that the publisher needs your work. Leave the editor enthusiastic about your potential contribution. Finish by expressing that you are looking forward to discussing your work with him/her, and provide all of your contact information (phone, address, fax, e-mail address) so that the editor can reach you easily. If you are querying via postal mail, it is helpful to include an SASE for the editor's reply. Many editors now accept e-mailed queries, which can speed up the process and save you postage; follow the same guidelines no matter your method of correspondence.

As with a cover letter, keep your queries brief and to the point but ensure that the editor has sufficient information to make a decision. Keep letters short and single spaced, and include full contact information. Table 3.1 shows an example of a query letter intended to gauge a publisher's interest in a proposed title (which was published in 2001 by ALA Editions as *Teaching the Internet in Libraries*). Note that it is short and to the point, yet in one page describes the prospective title and the author's qualifications to write it. You may also include a c.v. or résumé as well as writing samples to help the editor get a fuller picture of your background and writing ability.

Ensure also that you always query the current and appropriate acquisitions editor. The editor addressed in the 1999 query letter reproduced in the table, for example, had left ALA Editions by 2001. Do not address a query letter to: "Dear Editor" or "To Whom It May Concern"—take the time to find out the editor's name, and personalize your letter to him/her.

Also be sure to follow any directions provided by the press. ALA Editions, for example, requests a two- to three-page proposal (which was enclosed with the query in table 3.1); other book publishers may wish simply to see the query or will want a longer, more detailed proposal. Journals will request a query, or a query and an abstract, or just the completed manuscript.

The Query Process

You will wish to include clips of your previously published work with your query. These demonstrate your writing ability and show an editor that you have previous writing experience. If you are e-mailing a query, include the URLs where an editor can view samples of your work or include clips as attachments or as text within the body of your message. Contributor guidelines or calls for contributors will often outline how they prefer to receive clips via e-mail; note that many editors prefer not to receive attachments with initial queries due to the size of Word or PDF documents and the possibility of virus infection. Photocopies are acceptable when querying via postal mail; make sure, however, that they are legible and crisp. If your work appeared online, provide printouts and ensure that the entire current URL is included on the page so that an editor can easily visit the site.

If you wish to include your résumé with your query letter, be sure to rework and shorten it for this purpose. Include the qualifications and list the previous publications that are most pertinent to the work you are proposing. Leave off references if these are included in your résumé; the editor will not be offering you a job and will not need to contact these people.

When responding to your query, editors may suggest a change in direction or approach from that you have outlined in your letter. Their comments should allow you to create an article that is ultimately stronger and more appropriate for their publication. Use your best judgment here—if you believe that incorporating an editor's suggestions would change your proposed work into a piece you could not stand behind, politely decline and seek publication elsewhere. If you do receive a positive response to your initial query, especially if you since then have had little contact with the editor, remind him/her of this when turning in your final manuscript by including a cover letter thanking him/her for his/her interest in the piece.

Be sure when composing your query that you are willing and able to complete the final piece. The query outlines an article that you intend to write, not just an idea that you think might be interesting. Once an editor has accepted your query, he/she is counting on you to write the article.

When sending your query through postal mail, it may be tempting to send it certified mail so that you can ensure that the editor received it. Refrain. You do not want to make any extra work for your editor. By the same token, never call to pitch your ideas instead of sending a query letter. You do not want to force an editor into your schedule, and you definitely do not want to give him/her an easy excuse to turn you down.

Book Proposals

As with a query letter, the purpose of your book proposal is to outline and sell your idea to a potential publisher. Your proposal allows editors to evaluate your title in terms of its content, your qualifications, and the manuscript's sales potential. While the proposal outlines the book you intend to write, remain open to modifications and additions suggested by editors. They know the library audience and may suggest changes to make your manuscript better meet the needs of potential readers.

Elements of a Typical Proposal

While the specifics and order will vary, there are certain elements that nearly every publishing house will wish to see in your book proposal. These elements are aimed at helping acquisitions editors decide if your topic is broad enough to fill a whole book, if it will be marketable, and if it will be appropriate for their press. They will also need to find out if you are the best or most qualified person to write on this topic, get an idea of your writing ability, and ascertain both the originality of your idea and the competition it faces from other titles.

If publishers have not made their guidelines readily available, focus on the basic elements below when compiling your proposal for their house. Send your proposal in—to the appropriate editor!—with a brief cover letter. If you have previously sent a query and the editor asked to see a longer proposal, mention that you are sending it in response to his/her request, in order to jog his/her memory of your initial letter.

Begin with a simple title page, stating the proposed title of the work, your name as you wish it to appear on any published work, and your contact information. While the press may later want to go with a different title, still include one here. Make it clearly reflect the content of your proposed book.

Following the title page, the first element of a typical proposal asks for a short description of your proposed work. Keep this concise and to the point, and stay within the word count specified by the publisher (usually 300-500 words). Publishers are not looking for marketing hype at this point but merely for a description of your topic, your approach, and the scope of your book. They may wish to know what is unique about your proposed title; provide a sentence or two on what makes your project stand out. Also spell out the proposed length (generally in words rather than pages) of your work and the time you estimate it will take to complete the manuscript, as well as any additional content (screen shots, figures, photographs) you intend to include.

Acquisitions editors need to be able to take this descriptive statement to an editorial board meeting and have others understand immediately what your title will cover. While the acquisitions editor you initially contact may be convinced of the merits of your proposed work, he/she then has to convince her publishing house's editorial board—the board may overrule his/her excitement for reasons unrelated to the quality of your work, such as what they see as a low sales potential or a lack of clarity about the book's topic and focus. Take the chance the proposal provides to define your title for them.

Most publishing houses will also ask for an annotated table of contents, which lists the titles of and describes what will be included in each chapter. If you intend to divide the chapters into topical sections, indicate this in your table of contents as well. This element helps give an idea of whether your subject is broad enough to encompass an entire book. You will of course make changes or rearrange content while writing the actual book, but the table of contents in your proposal should fairly accurately reflect the topics you will be covering.

Academic presses may wish to see a thesis as well: what argument will you make in your work? What conclusions follow from your research? Your thesis, or argument, can be the defining element for a title which covers topics that have received previous attention in the library literature, especially if it shows that you have come to some unique conclusion. If you have not yet received all of the results from your research, you can instead show what is unique about your approach or about the questions you are asking. This helps answer the question as to why librarians and libraries will purchase your book instead of one of the others available on your subject. Presses publishing more scholarly material will also wish to receive a description of your research methodology.

Publishers will then wish to know about you—why are you the person to write this work? They will ask for a short biographical statement in which you should emphasize your knowledge of, research on, and any background in your proposed subject as well as any previous writing experience. Also emphasize in this section how your specific qualifications will help you promote the book. Do you have a Web site? Do you speak at conferences? Are you a columnist for a widely read professional journal?

At this point, many presses will also request a résumé or c.v., in which you can expand on your biographical statement with more detail on specific writing and work experiences. Here, do not supply the basic résumé you use when job-hunting, but tailor one specifically toward the subject of your title. Emphasize any experience you have that bolsters your claim to expertise on your subject and list full citations for any previous publications. If you intend to collaborate on this work, you will need to include a biographical statement and résumé for each author.

Some publishers will also request either a sample chapter from your proposed title or a sample of your previous writing to help them gauge your writing ability and style. Include your best work, and, if sending a previously published sample, try to include one that best matches the topic and tone of the book you wish to write. As with the clips you include with your queries, provide legible photocopies and/or URLs.

Any publisher will then wish to know about the potential market for your title. Who is going to buy your book, and why? Will it appeal to all librarians, or specifically to public librarians, systems librarians, or new librarians? Can it be used in a widely taught course? How big is the market, and why do these people need your book? Do you have a built-in audience for the title—do you regularly teach classes or make presentations at professional conferences, for example? The more specific you can be about numbers and audience, and the broader the appeal of your title, the better.

While information science titles, especially those published by academic presses, are somewhat less market dependent than general trade books, your publisher still needs to know that there is a market out there and that the book will sell. (Note that an inherently limited audience means that titles for librarians do not sell in huge numbers; one to two thousand copies is generally seen as a successful run.) Defining your audience will also be helpful as you begin to write the book, as you should always have your core reader in mind while writing.

This leads into the section on competing works. You will need to research what else has been written on your topic and be able to explain how your book differs from existing titles in scope, tone, or approach. (Begin your search for competing works in WorldCat, *Books in Print*, or in large online bookstores such as Amazon.com.) Purchase or interlibrary loan potentially competing titles and examine them closely so that you can describe accurately their differences from your own work. Concentrate on the last five years; publishers will be less interested in older, outdated works.

Table 3.2. Sample Proposal Guidelines, Scarecrow Press

1. Please provide a tentative descriptive title.

2. Tell us the subject matter, scope, and intended purpose of your manuscript. Please send us the introduction, table of contents, and summaries of the proposed chapters. A completed sample chapter that shows us your writing style, organizational techniques, and documentation would also be helpful. If your proposed book is a bibliography, we would like to see sample annotated entries.

3. Describe the research methods you will use and potential sources of data.

4. Please indicate whether the book will require photographs, illustrations, maps, appendix, index, etc.

5. When do you estimate the work will be completed? What length do you envisage for it?

6. What audience do you see for your work? What other books exist in this same subject area?

7. Has any part of your book been published previously and if so, where? If it is a doctoral dissertation, what changes are you proposing to prepare it for monograph publication?

8. Do you have written permissions to use material that may be copyrighted (illustrations, lengthy quotations from scholarly works, or any quotations from fiction or poetry)?

9. Please send us your c.v.

10. Please indicate how you will submit your manuscript if it is accepted: camera-ready or double-spaced manuscript pages. If you would be submitting double-spaced manuscript pages, you must submit disks containing the manuscript.

11. Please address all correspondence to Melissa Ray, Assistant Managing Editor, Scarecrow Press, 4501 Forbes Blvd., Suite 200, Lanham, Maryland 20706. Be sure to enclose a self-addressed envelope stamped with sufficient postage if you would like us to return the materials you send in.

If you cannot locate any works that seem to compete, publishers will wish to know why. You must be able to provide logical reasons why no one has previously addressed your topic because the first answer that comes to mind is that there is no actual need for a book on the subject. Be able to show that the time is now right for your topic or for your approach. Here you can also mention titles that complement your proposed work rather than directly competing with it, which can help show that there is a demand for similar (yet non-duplicative) material. Be sure to explain how your title fills a need unmet by these other works; explain why their audience should also become yours.

The last section of the proposal addresses delivery. How long will it take you to write the book? Are there any special requirements? What format can you deliver the manuscript in, and how long will it be? (Here provide an estimated word count rather than number of pages.) How will the title be organized? Will it include extra features, such as reproducible handouts, graphics, tables, or screen shots?

With your proposal you can also include supplementary material that helps support your qualifications and/or the need for the title. Send copies of articles you have written, especially those with some bearing on the subject of your proposed book. If there has been mention in the library press of a need that your title fills, copy the article and send it along, or at least cite it in your proposal. Here avoid overwhelming the editor with too much material—two or three articles should be sufficient.

Table 3.2 shows an example of typical book proposal guidelines. Note that each press will have its own requirements and may ask for different elements to be included.

The Proposal Process

You will often wish to query a publisher before sending in the full proposal to be sure that they are interested before spending the time and effort to mail your proposal package. Use the query letter to pique their interest, offering at the end of the letter to send the full proposal upon request. Have the proposal as close to ready as possible in case an editor does express interest; you do not want to make him/her wait. Query letters to library presses resemble those you would write to a journal: describe what you intend to write, why you are the one to do it, and who will want to read it. If your work would fit into an existing series by that publisher, say so—it will help them envision how your title will enhance their line.

This should go without saying, but always word process your book proposal and submit a clear (preferably laser-printed) printout in a standard 12-point font. Since proposals can be lengthy documents, number the pages for the publisher's convenience and include a running head consisting of the proposed title (or its first couple of words) and your last name. Refrain from stapling it, as an editor may need to make multiple copies for editorial meetings or for colleagues. Include a title page with your current contact information and an SASE for the publisher's reply—a standard envelope is sufficient if you just wish a reply; include sufficient postage to return the entire proposal if you would like it back.

You will also need to include a cover letter describing the contents of your proposal. As with a query, keep this brief, enthusiastic, and to the point. Also as with a query, keep both your cover letter and your proposal professional; all aspects of your work should reflect your professionalism and demonstrate your attention to detail. Mention if an editor has asked to see the full proposal—based on a query letter or at a conversation at a conference, for example—in order to jog his/her memory.

Be sure to follow guidelines in submitting both proposals and queries; for more on finding and following such guidelines, see chapter 2.

If you have previously established a relationship with an editor (if you have written for his/her press), you may not need to complete an entire proposal for your second title. The publisher now already has an idea of your credentials, your writing style, your ability to meet deadlines, and your work's sales potential. You may be able to sell a second—or third—title on the basis of a conversation, an e-mail, or a couple of pages of overview. Be able, however, to answer any questions that would come up in a typical proposal and to provide any of this material upon request.

Following Up

Editors are busy people and may not always respond to your queries and proposals as quickly as you might like. E-mail can also disappear into the ether, and postal mail may miss its destination.

If you fail to hear from an editor, wait a reasonable period of time (several weeks for a general publication, or up to several months for a library press or scholarly journal), and then write a very short and polite note. Mention that you are just writing to follow up on the proposal which was sent on [date], and that you are looking forward to hearing from them. Leave it at that. If you then receive no response, move on—some editors, as can people in any profession, lack manners or can be unreliable. You cannot spend unreasonable amounts of time waiting for a response which may never come. Send your query or proposal to the next publisher on your list.

Notes

1.   Susan Rabiner and Alfred Fortunato, *Thinking Like Your Editor: How to Write Great Serious Nonfiction—and Get It Published* (New York: W. W. Norton & Company, 2002): 62.

Chapter 4
Increasing Your Odds

While composing an effective query letter and/or book proposal is the single best means of getting your work accepted for publication, there are a number of simple yet commonly ignored steps you can take to improve your odds. Editors both want to find new authors to work with and need to find new material to publish, and are thrilled when they find writers who are distinguished by their attention to detail and professionalism. Remember that editors' success rests on constantly providing new and useful material to readers; publications and presses need writers as much as writers need them.

Unfortunately, newer and aspiring authors often fail to recognize the importance of seemingly minor details throughout the publication process (from spell check to proper manuscript formatting to familiarity with the journal), feeling that their work's strength should be inherently obvious. Successful writers realize, however, that failure to attend to detail can prevent editors from even getting to their content, and that professionalism and thoroughness can provide the "in" you need to get your work taken seriously.

In the following sections, you will find explanations of how to avoid common mistakes and how best to make your work stand out in a sometimes crowded field. At this point it might also be useful to turn to appendix B and examine the real-world publishing advice from editors at a variety of library publishing houses and journals; advice from other

Table 4.1. Tips and Tricks For Publishing Success

1. Let it rest. Resist the urge to turn in a manuscript the instant it is complete; put it away for at least a week so that you can read it over with a fresh eye before submitting.

2. Follow guidelines. Publishers provide these for a reason; ignore them at your peril.

3. Meet deadlines. Publishers are on a calendar and need time to put an issue together or to edit, print, and publish titles expected in a certain season.

4. Know your audience. Editors always have the target market of their journal or press in mind, and the most important factor in accepting or rejecting your manuscript is whether it meets the needs of that market.

5. Know your publishing outlet. Familiarity with the articles or titles it publishes allows you to conform to its requirements and style and prevents you from submitting manuscripts or queries that are clearly outside of its scope.

6. Deliver what you promise.

7. Learn to prize clarity and conciseness; avoid excessive jargon.

8. Ensure that your work makes a unique contribution to the literature.

9. Ensure that your research findings are statistically significant and clearly presented.

10. Write what you enjoy. If you try to write on subjects for which you feel little interest—let alone passion!—your apathy will inevitably show.

librarian authors on increasing your odds of being published is interspersed through this chapter.

Table 4.1 lists several tips for publishing success. While these may seem like simple common sense, they reflect editors' most common pet peeves about their interactions with authors—and potential authors. Assimilating these suggestions and making a habit of interacting professionally with editors can dramatically increase your odds of being published, regardless of the inherent quality of your writing.

Increasing Your Odds of Acceptance

As explained in the previous chapter, matching the content and style of your queries to particular publications' needs is of major importance. A common mistake beginning writers make is to blindly send a manuscript or query out to all the "big name" publications without taking the time to consider how their work fits into these journals and how they can tailor an inquiry to each. Pick one journal at a time, study its contents and needs, and customize your contact accordingly.

This is another instance where making a habit of reading regularly in the literature will pay off. Watch for editorials from journal editors discussing topics they would like to see submitted to their publication and for announcements of thematic issues. You will want to pick up on such editorials and announcements while they are still fresh, before the editor is overrun with ideas on his/her suggested themes or their timeliness has diminished.

Providence College Reference/Instruction Librarian Edgar Bailey shares an experience that helped him learn the importance of targeting publications' current needs and foci:

> Familiarize yourself with the types of articles published in the various journals. Submit to ones that focus on the area of your interest. Everyone would like to be published in *JAL* or *C&RL*, but there are many more specialized publications where you will have a better chance. Read the instructions to authors as well. I made the mistake of submitting an article to *RQ* just at the time when it was seeking to become more scholarly. Even though I wrote my article reporting a research project, I wrote it in the informal style which had previously characterized *RQ*. Although the article was ultimately accepted, I had to completely rewrite it to conform to the new policies.

Also consider sending your initial queries to smaller or lesser-known publications. While you may crave the recognition a well-known journal provides, publishing in smaller venues will both enhance your writing résumé and provide clips you can then send to larger journals. Prestigious peer-reviewed journals have a very high rejection rate since everyone wants to write for these publications. Working for smaller journals also allows you to practice your writing skills and can allow you to publish more controversial and more informal material than is acceptable at most of the bigger-name outlets.

Look at writing for smaller outlets just as you would approach applying for an entry-level position. When you start out in the library field, you may begin by working for a smaller library or in a less-than-ideal position; then a year or two later use your experience to move on to a location more suited to you. The same applies to publication in the library field—your experience with smaller publications or creating shorter pieces builds your résumé so that you are later ready to tackle larger projects. Experienced writer GraceAnne A. DeCandido suggests that beginning librarian authors "start small—book reviews and Letters to the Editor are an excellent place to begin." Massachusetts Board of Library Commissioners Consultant Shelley Quezada concurs: "Also, I think it is a great idea for folks to 'start small'—that is, begin by writing small articles for local state newsletters or contribute to your city or town newsletter. If they do not have one, then suggest beginning one. Writing . . . requires practice."

Alternatively, you may find that you actually prefer being a big fish in a smaller pond. You can spend your entire writing career happily writing for smaller or more informal publishing outlets, just as some information professionals prefer spending their whole library careers working in smaller institutions.

These smaller outlets include journals and newsletters published by your state library or library association. Such publications are always looking for contributors, and it can be easier to break into their pages than into national journals. They also may be more interested in descriptions of programs or projects in your library than larger journals, as you have the local angle working in your favor.

Whether submitting to local or national outlets, always keep any communication with editors professional and to the point. A query letter or manuscript full of typographical, grammatical, or spelling errors will be the kiss of death. Pay particular attention when composing e-mails to an editor, as it is easier to lapse into informality on-screen, and not all e-mail clients have spell check. Keep your manuscripts professional and clean as well. While a nicely formatted manuscript will not guarantee your acceptance, it can prevent your work from being rejected without being read. It will also prevent reviewers and editors from being biased against your work from the outset; they will not appreciate having to read a sloppy manuscript, and errors can easily distract them from the content of your writing. Take the opportunity to make a good first impression.

Working with Your Editor

Above all else, editors appreciate authors who work to deadline, work to guidelines, and deliver the work they originally promised. The easier you make your editor's job, the more appreciative he/she will be of your efforts.

Making your editor's job easy involves making all communication as clean, concise, timely, and complete as possible. You will find more tips on such details in chapter 5, but your main goal here is to avoid making him/her have to do any extra work. He/She should seldom need to ask you for clarification, track down material you should have provided, or work to interpret items you may have explained less than clearly. While every piece of writing will have minor issues requiring attention, major problems or lapses in detail are unnecessary and frustrating to editors.

Most importantly, follow any guidelines provided by your journal or publishing house. Failure to do so will make your editor think that you either did not bother to read their guidelines or cannot follow directions, neither of which makes you a person he/she will be keen on working with in the future. Realize also that many reviewers and editors, particularly at academic journals, are not compensated for their work (or are compensated very little). Refrain from wasting the time they are donating from their busy schedules by ignoring their guidelines and making others make your work fit a journal's style and requirements. (For more on finding and following guidelines, see chapter 2.)

If the guidelines note that you should follow a particular style manual while writing (such as the *Chicago Manual of Style* or the *Publication Manual of the American Psychological Association*), get your hands on a current copy of the appropriate guide and follow its instructions on manuscript preparation, capitalization, citation format, and so on. Note that some guides which have not been recently updated may not address the issue of how to format electronic citations. Check online to see if updated instructions have been posted on the publisher's Web site. These style manuals should be available at your library, or you may wish to invest in personal copies of the most commonly used guides for the publishing outlets you are targeting. If you format your manuscript incorrectly, the publisher will have to go through and make your work conform to house style—or will simply bump it back to you for revisions. See some sample bibliographic citations in table 4.2.

Table 4.2. Sample Bibliographic Citations

Below, find some simple bibliographic monograph citations in the styles of three commonly used guides. Note the differences in each that require attention to the preferences of each publishing outlet. Realize also that note formatting differs from bibliographic formatting, and that some guides will refer to creating a bibliography as constructing a reference list. Refer to specific guides for more detailed instructions and additional examples.

MLA Style Manual and Guide to Scholarly Publishing:

Nesbeitt, Sarah L., and Rachel Singer Gordon. *The Information Professional's Guide To Career Development Online.* Medford: Information Today, 2002.

Publication Manual of the American Psychological Association:

Nesbeitt, S. L., & Gordon, R. S. (2002). *The Information Professional's Guide To Career Development Online.* Medford, NJ: Information Today.

The Chicago Manual of Style:

Nesbeitt, Sarah L., and Rachel Singer Gordon. *The Information Professional's Guide to Career Development Online.* Medford, N.J.: Information Today, 2002.

Beyond formatting information, style guides also generally contain a great deal of useful content to assist authors. This can include instruction on clear writing style, information on designing and reporting on research, information on interpreting publishing contracts, manuscript preparation tips, and examples of using figures, graphics, and tables in your work. Spend some time familiarizing yourself with a guide and internalizing its instructions and suggestions; this will help strengthen your work and allow you to see how manuscripts in the field are generally prepared.

Be sure to meet any deadlines set by your editor. If you need an extension due to extenuating circumstances, inform him/her as far in advance as possible. (This does not mean the night before an article is due!) Lateness is both unprofessional and inconveniences your editor, who will likely have your article slated into a particular publication schedule or a book announcement scheduled to appear in a forthcoming catalog. Being late may also torpedo your chances of doing any further work for that publication or press, as you quickly gain a reputation for unreliability. If you find you are unable to complete the manuscript at all, tell your editor as soon as possible—don't wait until it is due because then he/she will need to scramble to fill the hole you have left in a journal issue or the publishing schedule.

Peter Rubie notes: "Deadlines are not really suggestions. It is the wise writer who always hands in his manuscript on time, or perhaps a little early if possible. . . . Don't wait to the last minute, it makes everyone's job twice as hard."[1] Your lateness on a book manuscript can also make a publishing house editor look bad when he/she has to make excuses for you to his/her marketing and production departments—remember, your acquisitions editor is the one who originally fought for your book idea; do not let him/her down.

When working with your editor, also do your best to be agreeable to his/her suggestions and comments. He/She has likely been doing this a long time, and incorporating his/her ideas will often strengthen your work—or at least increase your odds of publishing it. Genie Tyburski, Web manager, The Virtual Chase, advises: "The more flexible you are about editing, the better the publishing experience and relationship." Gustavus Adolphus College Professor Barbara Fister suggests that "if an article is accepted and you're lucky enough to get an editor who makes suggestions, take them seriously."

Editing, Rewriting, and Editing Again

One cardinal rule of publication is never to turn in the first draft of anything that you write. While a journal or publishing house will spend significant time editing your work, you never wish to subject your initial efforts to their tender mercies. Make your work as polished and error-free as possible before sending it off to your editor; he/she has more to worry about than dealing with obvious errors that you should have caught in your rewriting and editing efforts. (See chapter 5 for more on editing your work.)

This is not to say that you should spend your writing time constantly rewriting and second-guessing yourself. Get that first draft down on paper, then let it cool for a while before going back to it. While it is tempting to ride the momentum of finishing your draft and send it off immediately, resist that urge. Your work will be stronger if you take the time it needs, and your editor will thank you for it.

Once you have taken the time to get some distance from the first draft, go back and read it carefully. This is the time to polish your writing: locating spelling and grammatical errors, moving sections around so that they flow more naturally, adding material to clarify or strengthen your point, and rewriting sections as needed.

While the first draft of one project is incubating, you can always take some time to brainstorm ideas for another article, compose another query letter, or otherwise build on your writing momentum. Working on multiple projects can help keep your ideas fresh and help make writing a natural and consistent part of your career.

Defining Your Audience

A main component in the success of your writing will be your ability to define and write for a particular audience. Every piece of professional writing, from book reviews to articles to books, is addressed to a specific core group that will be able to make the best use of its content.

As Priscilla Shontz suggests: "Select an audience for your article. Write your article or publication to that audience. Some authors recommend visualizing a specific reader as you write so that you keep the article focused at your specific audience. This may help keep your writing style consistent and may ensure that you cover details that are important to your readers."[2]

Just as professional speakers often advise that presenters act and think as if they are talking one-on-one with a person rather than to an entire audience, it may help to target your writing as if you are talking to a colleague. Envision the typical reader for your book and write directly to her, just as if you were explaining your position one-on-one. Remember that your readers will not have done your research and will lack your specific background. So, you will need to provide sufficient information that a reader in your typical audience will easily be able to follow your logic and your arguments.

Defining the audience for an article is done in combination with settling on an outlet for your work. Ideally, your audience will closely match the target market of the journal in which you are publishing or the press that will bring out your book. If the ideal audience for your article or title differs too greatly, consider finding another publisher. Do not try to shoehorn your topic into a place it just does not fit; there are enough publishing outlets that you should be able to match your writing to its appropriate publisher. As one survey respondent emphasizes: "Know your audience and the style of the particular journal or newsletter for which you'd like to write."

Once you have defined your audience, remember through the entire writing process for whom you are writing. Your job here is to fulfill the needs of that audience through your work, answering their questions and providing material that will be helpful to their work, their own research, or their professional development. Along the way, any audience will be appreciative if you take the time to make your writing as clear, interesting, and readable as possible. While you may write for yourself, you publish for your readers.

Notes

1.   Peter Rubie, *The Everything Get Published Book* (Holbrook, Mass.: Adams Media Corporation, 2000): 192.
2.   Priscilla Shontz, *Jump Start Your Career in Library and Information Science* (Lanham, Md.: Scarecrow Press, 2002): 156.

Chapter 5
Writing and Editing Your Work

As librarians, we rely on written communication in many aspects of our daily work. From memos to dossiers, from grant applications to in-house or patron newsletters, the written word is a staple of our interactions with others. The challenge for aspiring librarian authors lies in extending the skills they have developed in carrying out these day-to-day tasks beyond their own libraries and using them to create effective pieces of professional writing. Everything you have learned as a writer will now come in handy, from your days pounding out papers in graduate school to your recent attention to creating an effective report to your board. Those who wish to write for the profession, however, will need to develop some additional techniques and learn to look at the act of writing from a somewhat different perspective.

Professional writing, from its audience to its length, differs from other forms of written communication. Your audience consisting largely of other librarians, for example, means that library jargon and the assumption of a certain commonality of background will inform your work. If you are writing peer-reviewed, academic articles, your writing builds on research you have done in the field and has certain requirements as to tone and format (see chapter 7). Articles or proposals need to conform to the needs and wants of editors and audiences.

Becoming a writer of professional work requires developing the mindset of a professional writer. This means cultivating attention to all

ils involved in creating a piece of writing, from finding the time
/ regularly to creating a professional-looking manuscript.

Time Management

One of the most difficult tasks for beginning writers is mastering the art of managing their writing time effectively. It is all too easy to lose focus or to become distracted by other issues, until the weeks have flown by and you find yourself under deadline pressure—or, worse, you find that you never even got around to submitting your idea to a publisher, and now someone else has beaten you to it.

The best way to overcome procrastination is to get yourself in the habit of writing each and every day. Set yourself a realistic goal of five hundred words a day, one typed page a day, one hour a day, or whatever amount is manageable given your other commitments. Even if this target is relatively small to begin with, your daily writing will add up and will get you in the habit of *being* a writer. And, even if you end up discarding or rewriting much of this daily work, you are exercising your writing muscles. It is also generally much easier to revise and extend the writing you have created than to face starting from scratch. Do not worry at this point about how good your writing is, how grammatically correct it is, or any of the nitpicky issues that distract you from getting your thoughts down on paper (or screen). Worry first about content; form comes later.

Another way to jump start the writing process is to begin your work on a given article or manuscript with the chapter or section with which you are most comfortable. You need not feel compelled to start at the beginning and write straight through; start where you are strongest and work backwards, forwards, or outwards from there. Worry about the cohesion of your writing during the later editing stage, where you will find yourself reworking, rewriting, and reorganizing much of your initial content.

Your daily writing will be both more useful and easier to do if you are working toward a particular goal, after you have had a query or proposal accepted by a publisher. Each daily chunk of writing you produce then gets you that much closer to your target of a finished draft. (If you write just five hundred words, or approximately two double-spaced pages, a day, you will complete a draft of an entire sixty-thousand-word book manuscript in four months!) Set yourself deadlines, and do your best to stick to them. Self-imposed deadlines can also help if you have a tendency toward perfectionism; realize that your work will never fully seem "finished," but set a point where you will need to call it done. You can then reward yourself with time off between projects, or spend this time researching or catching up on what is new in your field. (However, consciously limit this "time-out" period, so that your writing muscles do not lose their tone.)

You may find yourself better able to churn out this daily writing if you begin by creating an outline of your article or book project. (Books here can be somewhat easier, as you have already done some of this work when your created the annotated table of contents for your proposal.) Each writer works differently; some create a detailed outline of each section of their work before beginning to write, others may scribble notes on scratch cards, while some may merely keep a rough outline in their heads and be able to just sit down and write. Do not force yourself to create a formal outline if you do not work well this way. However, if you find yourself stuck or your writing seems aimless, an outline may help give you back your focus.

One technique that proves successful for many authors is to take some time to create a mental picture of their final goal. Picture your completed manuscript or your finished article; envision how it will look when it is printed out. Working backwards from the point of a finished manuscript, think about what you needed to do just before completing your goal—perhaps you contacted copyright holders for reprint permission, or did final editing on the PC before printing your manuscript out. What did you have to do just before that? Did you organize your chapters, then do the actual writing? Before that, you likely researched your topic or identified people to interview. Before that, you brainstormed topics and identified the best places to submit your idea. Working backwards from a clear image of your final goal can help you identify all the steps you need to take to achieve that goal in the order you need to take them.

As you continue writing, you will discover the methods that work the best for you.

Finding Time

When trying to find the time to write, take advantage of any special opportunities provided by your employer. Some academic libraries, for example, offer release time for research and writing to librarians who have put in a certain number of years, or encourage them to devote part of their workday to professional activities such as writing. Many working librarians, however, will not be so lucky.

You may need to rearrange your day and set aside a specific block of time each morning or evening for your writing. Get up an hour earlier each morning, or cut out some of the time you would otherwise spend watching TV each night. Experiment to see what works best for you and fits well into your schedule. If you wish to write regularly for professional publication, make the effort to write every day—whether you feel like it or not. Otherwise it becomes easy to put it off, and you will find that weeks or months fly by without you having accomplished anything.

Above all, do not get into the habit of convincing yourself that you lack the time to write and allowing yourself to fall behind in your goals. Like any worthwhile activity, good writing requires a certain amount of discipline, and saying you have no time usually just means that you have made other activities a priority. If you wish merely to write an occasional article, this is fine—you do not need to be as focused. If you intend to make writing for publication a regular part of your professional life, though, you will need to develop a continuing commitment. Decide if writing is important to you beyond the immediate bit you may need to publish for tenure or promotion. If it is, allot yourself the time it takes to do it well.

Take advantage of any blocks of time that become available to you. Carry a pen and pad with you for those times when you are stuck on the train or waiting for an appointment, and use this time for brainstorming, jotting down notes, or even writing whole articles. (These "found" bits of time are best for nonacademic writing, editing, or note-taking that you can accomplish away from the majority of your reference/research materials.)

If an idea strikes you at work and you lack the time to sit down and develop it fully, jot yourself a quick e-mail or leave yourself a voicemail to jog your memory later. Make note of ideas as they occur because they have an annoying tendency to disappear when you try to recall your flash of inspiration later. If you want writing for publication to become a regular part of your professional life, then consciously make it a regular part of your daily life as well. The more writing you do, the more you are exercising your creative muscles, and the easier the writing process becomes.

Organization and Research

You will find that the process of writing and researching falls into place much more easily if you have taken the time to organize your working environment on an ongoing basis. As you read the library literature, copy or make note of articles and ideas that are relevant to your own work. Start developing a personal library of useful material that you can turn to as needed during the writing process, organized in whatever manner makes the most sense to you and to the way you work.

Extend this organization to your writing as well. Your writing stands a better chance of being published—and read!—if you present your ideas in an orderly progression. Ensure that each sentence, paragraph, and section naturally follows its predecessor and builds on the concepts you have previously presented. Lay out the structure for your book or article before you begin writing; it will help you stay organized and help your writing flow. Break it up with headings and subheadings that clearly describe the writing that follows.

Make research an ongoing process. One common trap is thinking that all research must be completed before you can even begin writing—while librarians of all people should realize that research is always a process rather than a clearly demarcated project. Many of us have a tendency toward perfectionism and feel that digging further is sure to turn up the perfect article or statistic to bolster our work. This can bog you down in a never-ending quest. Learn to look at research as a constant activity; you can always go back and add to or modify your work as you encounter new ideas or uncover new facts.

As part of this ongoing process, realize that your professional writing occurs in conversation with your colleagues'. Others' articles, monographs, letters, and other writing define their role in the ongoing conversation, and, as you begin to read more widely in the field and to collect material for your personal library, you will also begin to see gaps in the conversation where your voice may fit. Make a note of these gaps, either mentally or in your personal files, as sources of inspiration for future articles.

Do not neglect material outside of the library field. Our profession is necessarily multidisciplinary and informed by others' work in fields from education to computer science to futurism, and ideas from other fields can provide a new way of thinking and spark your own creativity. Everything you read is potential fodder for future writing; everything you read helps inform your own thinking and provide the background for your work.

Do realize, however, that much of your background research needs to be completed before you begin your actual writing. While it does not have to be "finished," your research lays the foundation for your writing and you will find it much more difficult to organize and write an article (let alone a book!) if you have not done your homework ahead of time. Utilize resources such as *LISA* and *Library Literature*, as well as any other indexes to which your institution subscribes, to locate other articles on your topic. Take advantage of the ability to e-mail articles to yourself; start an e-mail box for your current project for easy referral. As you do your research, jot down notes or begin creating an outline—you may find that your work naturally organizes itself!

Details, Details, Details

You will want to use a standard word processor such as Microsoft Word to compose all of your professional writing. If you do not have access to a copy of Word, note that many other programs can save in Word (.doc) format or Rich Text Format (.rtf), which many publishers will ask for. This is important in that editors who receive your work electronically must be able to open and edit it easily; do not make them go out of their way to convert your text into a readable format. Corel's WordPerfect software and downloadable open source alternatives such as Open Office (http://www.openoffice.org) or Sun's StarOffice (http://wwws.sun.com/software/star/) can each save in Word format, and these may be more affordable if you are on a tight budget.

If you are more comfortable composing your initial drafts in longhand, do so. At some point, however, you will need to transfer your material into your word processor, both for ease in editing and to create a professional manuscript to turn into your editor. Always back up your work; try to become obsessive about having multiple copies. You need to be able to recover instantly from a hard drive or computer crash. If you are comfortable doing so and have the storage space available to you, you may wish to keep a backup copy at work or otherwise "off-site" from your home PC. Or, attach your working files to a message and e-mail your current projects to yourself for backup, or invest in a Zip drive or some other form of removable storage for backup. Do not keep the only copy of your work on floppy disk—although easily portable, floppies are an extremely impermanent medium.

Make sure that your manuscript conforms to the publisher's specifications, down to details such as font size, spacing after periods, capitalization, formatting of footnotes, and so on. Do not simply assume that editors will do this formatting and proofreading for you. Remember, if you make their job easier, they will be more open to working with you in the future. Also stay within the publication's word count; do not assume that a journal can make the cuts for you—they may, but they may do so begrudgingly, and may make cuts that do not do justice to your work.

If the publisher fails to specify formatting for your work, follow these simple guidelines:

- Use a 12-point, standard font such as Times New Roman for all manuscripts and correspondence.
- Single space all correspondence, double space between paragraphs.
- Double space all manuscripts.
- Use one-inch margins all around.
- Do not staple anything.
- Single space after all periods and other punctuation. (The old convention of double spacing after periods went out with typewriters.)
- Use standard white copy/printer paper.
- Include a running head on each page listing the manuscript's author and title, and number your pages.
- Make sure that your printer has a fresh ink cartridge or toner. If using an inkjet printer, ensure that it prints crisply. If your inkjet tends to smudge, bring your manuscript on disk to a copy shop or to your local public library and print it out using a laser printer.
- Ensure that any photocopies are legible and clear. Again, if the machine at your workplace is less than satisfactory, pay the nice people at the copy shop to do it for you.

Make your manuscripts look standard and straightforward; this is not the time to get creative with fonts, design, or paper.

Editing Your Work

You will be the first—and hopefully strictest—editor of your own work.

This should go without saying, but always spell check and proofread your work before turning it in to an editor. (You can safely ignore Word's grammar-checking capability, which often creates more problems than it solves.) Do not, however, rely on spell check to catch all of your errors; be sure to put your work aside for a few days after finish-ing it so that you can read and proofread with a fresh eye. Avoid obses-sive editing during the writing process itself. Get a draft down on paper before going back to rewrite and edit so that you do not get bogged down in the editing process and never finish the manuscript itself.

Also get at least one other person to go over your writing, as you may be too close to what you have written to notice typographical and other errors. As one survey respondent advises: "In addition to select-ing a topic you are interested in, I'd recommend that you get someone who is brutally honest with you to critique your work." Editors can and will reject an otherwise appropriate work on the basis of poor proof-reading, their natural suspicion being that these surface errors reflect an underlying sloppiness in the work itself.

Like the writing process, the editing process helps you clarify your own thinking on the issues you are writing about. Going back over your own work lets you make it say what you really mean to say, and lets you see where your ideas may be unclear or your research sloppy. Fix these issues before turning the manuscript in, better you deal with them than your editor. As Abby Day puts it:

> There's nothing like seeing your idea in black and white to make you take it seriously. Did I really say that? Am I sure about this?
> Usually, to get it right, you have to get it wrong first. To achieve a finished draft, you have to go through a first and second draft. Manufacturers call it concurrent engineering; working it out as you go, restructuring, revising, adding, subtracting—in other words, learning.[1]

Writing is a constant process of writing, editing, rewriting, and editing again: each iteration making your draft stronger and your thinking clearer.

Cultivating Clarity

Beginning writers, especially academic writers, often labor under the misconception that professional writing is inherently obtuse. While an unfortunate proportion of scholarly writing has a tendency toward im-penetrability, this is by no means necessary. Obfuscation for obfusca-tion's sake often signifies a writer who lacks confidence in his/her own abilities and tries to mask that fact with jargon and verbosity.

You wish to write not to impress but to explain. When composing your article or book manuscript, you are not only addressing your editor (or tenure committee!), you are writing for an audience of other librarians whom you wish to inform and/or influence. Editors seek work that will be suitable to their defined audience, which is work that that audience can make use of and will find readable.

You should strive for clarity when editing your work. Learn to be fair yet ruthless when editing your own writing; removing unnecessary verbiage and jargon makes you a stronger writer. Now is not the time to lengthen your manuscript through extensive adjectives or roundabout descriptions. If you find yourself needing to resort to such measures, perhaps you have chosen the wrong outlet for your work. Investigate publications seeking shorter articles, or allow yourself the room to expand on your topic and add content instead of cluttering up your writing with superfluous additions.

Examine your writing on a printed page. If merely looking at a printout exhausts your eyes, you need to simplify your style. Go back and break paragraphs into shorter logical chunks. Add headings to break up your prose and to group relevant sections together. Vary the lengths of your sentences; try reading a section of your work aloud to see if the breaks seem natural. Remember the need for white space, which is especially important if you are writing a shorter article or composing work for an online audience. The more readable your work, the more likely it will be read, digested, cited, and commented on by your peers.

Getting Help

You may wish also to peruse more general writing-related resources, of which there are many. Although some of the advice found in these Web sites, books, and articles is less relevant to librarians, information on reading contracts, writing concisely, time management, and so on is applicable to authors in any field.

If you work in a public or academic library, you should have ready access to any number of guides for writers in your own institution's collection. Realize that much of the advice in these guides on agents, coming up with popular topics and so on is less applicable, and skim to glean the pertinent information for you. If you are in an academic institution, look up guides to scholarly publishing; much of their advice for professors and other faculty will be equally pertinent to you. You may

Table 5.1. General Writing-Related Web Sites

Internet Resources for Writers
    http://www.internet-resources.com/writers/

Publishing Law Center
    http://www.publaw.com

Writer's Pocket Tax Guide
    http://www.foolscap-quill.com/wptg2002.html

Writers Write
    http://www.writerswrite.com

WritersDigest.com 101 Best Web Sites for Writers
    http://www.writersdigest.com/101sites/2002_index.asp

WritersWeekly.com
    http://www.writersweekly.com

Writing-World.com
    http://www.writing-world.com

---

also wish to look into the associations for researching librarians listed in table 7.3, as well as the research methods guides in table 7.2.

Be sure to take advantage of any resources available to you. Take every opportunity to improve your writing, editing, and researching capabilities.

Notes

1.   Abby Day, *How to Get Research Published in Journals* (Hampshire, England: Gower Publishing, 1996): 5.

Chapter 6
Networking and Collaboration

It has been said that writing is a lonely business—well, librarians turn that adage on its head. The peculiar strength of librarianship lies in the commitment of its practitioners to facilitating the free flow of information, and professional publication in the field is no different. You will find that your colleagues, especially other authors, are generally willing to share ideas and expertise, read over drafts, provide quotes, complete surveys, write forewords, endorse books, and collaborate with you on research projects, articles, and monographs. This cooperative spirit, of course, does create a reciprocal responsibility for you when one of your peers asks for ideas, assistance, or collaboration; be equally willing to participate in or lend assistance with others' projects.

For academic librarians, the peer review process itself serves as a certain form of networking. Even "blind" reviewers with whom you do not interact directly are providing feedback on your work, often including suggestions for improvement or ideas on directions your arguments and research could have taken.

The following sections will describe various methods of networking with others, focusing on topics such as finding others with whom to network, creating and interpreting useful surveys and questionnaires, eliciting quotes and interviews from your fellow librarians, and finding and working with an article or book coauthor.

All of your networking efforts go toward making your voice part of the continuing conversation that underlies our professional literature, and the health of this cooperative conversation depends on many voices participating. As GraceAnne A. DeCandido advises: "Do it. Make your voice heard. Become part of the cultural memory of librarianship. All library work is collaborative, and library writing especially so."

Collaborating

If you are just starting out in library publication, or if you are more comfortable with the idea of being able to bounce ideas off of others than you are with the thought of working solo, you may wish to find a coauthor for your article or book project. The convenience of electronic communication means that you can easily extend your search for a collaborator to include geographically remote colleagues. (See more on online communication in chapter 11.) Even if you are not geographically separated, e-mail provides a convenient method of sharing drafts and comments and can provide a written record of your progress.

Collaboration can help you to jump start the writing process and to keep yourself writing. One academic librarian notes that: "Finding a coauthor is also a good way to keep you focused and keep the writing process moving along, as you now have a responsibility to another person." Feeling accountable to your coauthor can help keep you on track—and your collaborator will hopefully feel the same way.

Working with a coauthor also allows you to ease into tackling longer projects, such as a book manuscript. Sharing the workload with another person helps the process seem less intimidating and may allow you to complete the writing more quickly. You can concentrate more closely on your own sections of the work rather than trying to focus on every chapter in the book, which allows you more time for research and may strengthen your writing. Further, the opportunity to share ideas with your coauthor throughout the entire process leads to a more useful final manuscript that incorporates both of your efforts.

Writing with a more experienced colleague also allows you the chance to ease into the process of professional publication, benefiting from others' experiences. Trudi Jacobson, coordinator of User Education Programs at the University at Albany, suggests: "If you can, coauthor your first piece with a more experienced librarian who has already published and knows the ropes. He or she can guide you this first time, and you will be less hesitant to do it on your own in the future."

While working with another author offers a number of benefits, be very careful when choosing a collaborator to pick someone whose working habits, writing style, and attitude mesh well with yours. If you are most comfortable planning, outlining, and working steadily on a project until its completion, for example, you may not want to work with a coauthor who prefers to procrastinate and produce most of the work in large bursts just before deadline. If you are proposing to collaborate on a peer-reviewed article, you may not want to work with a coauthor whose only writing experience is in more informal publications. You will likely be uncomfortable working with or find yourself arguing with a coauthor whose opinions or conclusions in his/her previously published work differ dramatically from your own. Consider these issues carefully before agreeing to any collaboration.

Start by seeing what work your potential coauthor has previously done; get an idea of his/her writing style and topics of interest. This is another good reason to both read widely in the professional literature and to build strong networks before you need them. Keep track of other librarians working on similar subjects or whose approach seems to complement yours. If you have in the past taken the time to strike up conversations or initiate e-mail exchanges with authors whose work you have found of interest, then you have a pre-existing relationship to build on when it comes time for you to find a collaborator. Or, others may find your exchanges of interest and approach you first with the idea of collaborating on a project.

When you do decide to work with a collaborator, there are a number of issues you must agree on before proceeding with the project. These include:

- Whose name will come first on the finished work?
- How will you share expenses, if any?
- How will you split the proceeds of a book project or an article you anticipate receiving payment or royalties for?
- How will you divide the workload (including writing, research, and editing)?
- Will copyright be registered jointly?
- How (and how often) will you communicate with one another during the writing process?
- Where do you each envision submitting the work?
- Who will take responsibility for communicating with your editor?
- If collaborating on a book, how do you each intend to help publicize the title?
- Will you both be comfortable presenting on the topic, or can you envision copresenting, if invited to do so?

Discuss and resolve such issues at the outset rather than leaving them to work themselves out as you go along; never sign a contract with any publisher until these issues are settled. It is not a publisher's responsibility to resolve problems between collaborators.

Be careful of collaborating with friends—if this partnership for any reason goes awry, you do not wish to lose a friendship as well. The same applies to collaborating with coworkers—while your proximity can improve communication, you will need to continue to work together after your writing project is finished. On the plus side, however, you likely already have a good idea of the work styles and approach of both friends and coworkers. This knowledge can help forestall later surprises.

Be sure to agree in advance on what will happen if one coauthor neglects to complete his or her share of the work, and think about how your working together now might affect future solo competing projects. You may wish even to formalize and sign a separate collaboration agreement with your coauthor in order to protect both of your interests, spelling out each of your rights and responsibilities when it comes to your joint work.

If a colleague asks you to collaborate on his/her project, ask these same sorts of questions. Make sure the scope of work, form of credit, and amount of payment are explicitly spelled out before beginning to work together. Make sure that this is someone you will be able to work comfortably with for an extended period of time, especially if you are agreeing to collaborate on a book manuscript. You may be working together for months, if not years!

When you begin working on your book or article manuscript, your first step is to decide together on an appropriate division of labor and on self-imposed deadlines for each stage of the project. This may require one or both of you to be more organized than normal. Be responsible for living up to your side of the bargain by adhering to deadlines and keeping in close communication with your coauthor.

The most difficult part of collaboration can be merging your writing styles and giving your manuscript the cohesion and clarity it needs. You may wish to alternate writing sections or chapters and then each edit/add to the other's work. Make sure to have a third party read and comment on your manuscript before turning it in to an editor; an outside perspective can help you see where the differences in your styles are noticeable.

Conferences and Workshops

To make the most of your time at an association conference or workshop, plan ahead as much as possible. Conferences provide the opportunity to attend sessions on being published in the profession or on your topic of interest, as well as to network with others in the field. If you are able to find sessions on your topic, make time to talk with the presenter afterwards—this is a built-in networking opportunity with someone who is doing similar work, and may lead to a contact, a correspondent, or a collaborator. During the talk, think of an insightful question or comment with which you can begin a conversation. If you lack the time to stick around after the session, e-mail your reaction to the presenter a couple of days later or when you return home.

Also be alert to more informal opportunities to network with others at association events. Talk with others who are attending the same sessions or stopping at the same vendor booths, or go to meet-and-greets held by relevant association subgroups. The more contacts you make at a conference, the bigger the network you have to draw on in all stages of your writing career.

At larger meetings, take time to talk to publishers at exhibit booths. Share what you are working on, especially if your ideas dovetail well with the focus of their press or publication. This may lead to writing opportunities, as publishers recognize the networking potential of conferences as clearly as librarians. Northeast State Technical Community College Librarian Chrissie Anderson Peters describes the impetus for her first article in library literature:

> I had just attended my first ALA and Charlie Fox of *Library Mosaics* struck up a conversation with me in the Exhibits Hall about all the ribbons I had on my name tag. As a student member of ALA, I believe in "test-driving" any division or round table that might interest me, so I have a better idea of where I want to spend my non-student dues after I complete my MSIS. . . . As I explained this theory of membership to him, he encouraged me to write a piece for *Library Mosaics* about my experiences. So I did.

Realize, however, that editors searching for potential authors at conferences and related venues may have very specific ideas as to what they want these authors to write about. Consider whether an "assigned" topic from one of these editors truly strikes your interest before saying yes—you may be technically able to write on the subject, but your lack of passion for the topic will be apparent in your work.

You should also be on the lookout for opportunities to share your work and learn from others' research during professional conferences. ALA's Library Research Round Table (LRRT), for example, invites attendees to ALA Annual to share the results of their research by presenting their prepublication papers during scheduled LRRT forums. Presentations are followed by discussion, and papers are selected based on the significance of the research, the quality of their methodology, and their potential to fill gaps or build on previous studies in the field.

Your networking activities and writing activities in this way reinforce each other throughout your career. Every opportunity to network in person with others provides another opportunity to find a collaborator or an editor and to be exposed to new ideas that will enhance your work.

Surveys and Interviews

Well-designed surveys and interviews are useful in providing material both for research articles and for those appearing in general library publications. In general journals, readers are always interested to find out what their peers are thinking and saying about a topic of interest. In an academic environment, surveys provide a ready source of data for you to analyze. They are also a helpful source for quotes, statistics, and other material that help add interest and substance to your writing.

To aid your return rate, remember to keep any surveys short and your questions clear and on-topic for your survey population. You can either choose to mail or hand out a written survey to a predetermined group of participants (either other librarians or members of the general public), or open it up by posting it on library-related mailing lists and Web sites. Your choice here depends on the scope and purpose of your questionnaire. Ask targeted questions that can be answered briefly and keep your survey manageable—the longer and more complicated it seems, the fewer people will take the time to answer.

If you choose to conduct your survey via postal mail, include an SASE for each participant. Online questionnaires that post the results from a Web-based form directly into your e-mail box are simple to set up and can be more easily managed, but you may miss potential respondents who spend less time online or who are less willing to fill out surveys on screen. Further, a generally announced online survey lacks a certain rigor since you are not screening for a statistically valid and representative sample; you may wish to reserve this method for gathering data or quotes for nonacademic work. (For information on structuring a statistically valid survey, consult a library research methods guide; see the recommended reading list in table 7.2 in chapter 7 for suggestions.)

In a more general questionnaire, ask questions that you and your potential readers will find of interest. After basic questions such as name, contact information, sex, and so on, you can open your questions up to try and elicit opinions, ideas, and examples from your respondents. This type of survey lends itself to open-ended questions, which respondents can answer at length if desired. You can combine these open-ended questions with basic yes/no responses or with "scale" questions which ask respondents to choose among differentiated responses (strongly agree, agree, neutral, disagree, and strongly disagree, for example).

Interviews are similar in that you will need to develop a set of questions for your interviewees which will elicit both useful responses for your work and interesting and informative responses for your readers. Interviews can be conducted in person, over the phone, in writing, or electronically via e-mail. Each method presents its own advantages and drawbacks; in-person interviews, for example, run the risk of the interviewer "coaching," biasing, or otherwise influencing the respondent, while written interviews lack the flexibility and spontaneity of other methods and do not present the opportunity for the interviewer to clarify potentially ambiguous questions. Try to avoid showing your completed interview to the interviewee prior to publication to avoid endless rounds of clarification and rethinking.

For certain types of papers, you may also wish to conduct focus group interviews. It will generally be easier to tape-record these moderated small-group sessions, which should be comprised of a representative sample of the population you are trying to examine. Because of scheduling conflicts and the varied willingness of people to participate in such forums, however, it is difficult to use focus group results in a research paper—this method may be more useful to get a "feel" for certain issues or to get a sense of the prevailing patron sentiment on a library program or service that you can then either act on or take to your administration.

You might find that some peer-reviewed publications are less likely to be seeking articles reporting the results of surveys, feeling that this type of research has been overdone. Before embarking on a survey project, review the requirements and leanings of the publications to which you are considering submitting your results. You may also wish to supplement the data collected from your survey with other methods of data collection.

Advice and Feedback

Getting advice and feedback from your colleagues is an essential step in creating a publishable manuscript. You will need to get up the courage to share your work with colleagues prior to its publication. Getting another person's point of view and comments on your manuscript before submitting it to a journal or library press can save you from embarrassing mistakes in front of your editor.

Incorporating others' suggestions into your work can strengthen your arguments and your writing. As one survey respondent suggests: "I counsel a lot of librarians who are preparing to do research, write, and submit manuscripts. My constant advice is to have colleagues and friends read over your drafts. I myself have benefited enormously from 'volunteer' editorial comments, and I find that people are often flattered to be asked. Don't be inhibited about sharing your early, rough efforts. You will learn a lot from the feedback."

You are often too close to your own writing to see where changes or clarification may be needed. See if you can develop a relationship with another librarian author, agreeing to look over and make suggestions on each other's work. It is important here to pick someone who will be honest in critiquing your writing; you are not looking here for a friend to boost your ego but instead for someone to provide constructive feedback that will allow you to produce a stronger piece of writing. Some librarians prefer to solicit input from colleagues in different fields in order to incorporate various points of view, while others prefer to exchange ideas and manuscripts with colleagues in their own institutions or with others addressing similar issues. Whichever you prefer, find someone to read your writing whose opinion you trust. Look for mentors and colleagues to provide first input before submitting your work to an editor's tender mercies. Consider starting a writing support group to critique and comment on each other's work.

Overall, collaborating and interacting with others is an integral part of your successful career as a writing librarian. Professional writing, just like any other professional work, cannot take place in a vacuum.

Chapter 7
The Academic Environment

Academic librarians face particular publication challenges. They may be required to publish in order to achieve tenure or promotion within their institution, for example, and their writing must pass through a peer-review process prior to its publication in refereed journals. Academic writing, further, shares a number of characteristics not usually found in articles in the more general library press, including adherence to a strict research methodology. When beginning to plan out a scholarly article or monograph, it will be useful to think back to any research methods coursework you may have had in library school. Also consult the research methods guides listed in table 7.2 for further background.

Beyond its importance to tenure and promotion, academic writing provides an outlet for you to publish your research and get it read by others in the field. While most of this interchange takes place via journal articles, consider also the possibility of writing a book for an academic press if your subject demands a more in-depth treatment. (For more on book proposals, see chapter 3; for more on writing a book, see chapter 9.)

If you do intend to write for the academic environment, be sure to keep up with the scholarly literature in your field. Read the major journals and watch for new titles that address your interests. Making a habit of reading the literature regularly is the best way to learn about academic writing and to familiarize yourself with the types of articles that get published in peer-reviewed journals. Reading the literature gives you examples to emulate, and shows you which journals are often cited and often read. This is important not only because it provides you with the background knowledge you need in order to yourself communicate effectively in the academic environment but also because it allows you to get a picture of what is being published in the field before you inadvertently duplicate others' efforts in your own work.

Always survey the relevant literature before submitting a query or book proposal so that you do not seem ignorant of developments in your own field. Academic journals, particularly, seek articles that make a new contribution to the field, which means doing original research and avoiding merely rehashing others' work. Note that peer-reviewed articles often also contain the author's suggestions for further research that can be done on a topic, which can help inspire your own research efforts in a related yet nonduplicative area.

Peer Review

Articles that appear in a peer-reviewed (or refereed) journal have been evaluated by one or more experts in the field prior to publication. Reviewers are often members of the journal's editorial board, but a journal may also turn to experts as outside reviewers if your topic is somewhat specialized or if the review board is small or overloaded. After an article is reviewed, it will either be accepted, rejected, or returned with suggestions for revisions you need to make before it can be accepted for publication at that journal.

If you are asked to revise your work, the revised article will reenter the review process when you submit it for the second time. It will at that point either be accepted or rejected—or returned for yet more revisions. If an editor invites you to revise and resubmit your article, do so, unless the suggested changes would completely distort your meaning. The proposed revisions may make your work stronger, will make it more appropriate for the particular publication, and will give you a good chance at getting your work accepted. Editors would not ask you to revise your work if they thought it lacked potential; a revision request indicates a true interest in publishing a revised version in their journal. Further, most manuscripts are not accepted on the first try; academic authors can reasonably expect to be asked to make revisions prior to acceptance for publication.

If a manuscript is sent back to you for revisions, the editor will give you a set period of time to make these changes before the revised version is due back. Stay within this deadline; the editor may already be envisioning where your revised manuscript fits in the journal's publication schedule. If you cannot in good conscience make all of the suggested changes, write to the editor and explain exactly which changes you are willing to make and which you feel would dilute your meaning or weaken the manuscript, and why. He/She will either accept your compromise or require that you make all suggested changes, in which case you always have the option of withdrawing your work from consideration and submitting it to another publication. Consider your objections carefully before writing your editor to ensure that they are valid and that you are not just put out that the reviewer voiced concerns about your original submission.

The peer-review process generally lengthens the time it takes for a submitted piece to be published in a journal. Many journals allow six weeks to three months just for the review process, and at some it can take over a year from its initial submission for your article to appear in print. If the timeliness of your work is an issue, you may wish to consider the length of the entire publication process before submitting your work to particular journals, and instead look into alternate publishing venues.

Many peer-reviewed publications employ a "double-blind" process in which neither the writer nor the reviewer is made aware of the other's identity. If you are asked to submit multiple copies of your paper and to only include your name on the cover sheet, this is generally a sign that the double-blind method is employed. This may or may not be stated in the journal's description and/or guidelines. Also realize that the library world is a small one, and that well-read editorial board members may be able to recognize the style, research methods, and topics of well-known authors—making the double-blind process less than "blind" in some cases.

Publication in peer-reviewed journals is an important part of the tenure process in many institutions, where librarians are often held to the same publish or perish standard as other faculty members. Some academic libraries, particularly large research institutions belonging to ARL (Association of Research Libraries) even have publication quotas for professional librarians. Librarians at these universities are required to publish a certain number of articles in peer-reviewed journals before they can be considered for tenure. In other cases, peer-reviewed publication is one factor in the tenure/promotion process, or publication in academic journals will carry more weight during this process than will publication in more general outlets. The promotion and tenure guidelines at your institution should spell out these requirements, but also be sure to talk to your peers who have already gone through the process. They can tell you the unofficial standards and personal preferences of your promotion/tenure committee.

Peer-reviewed publication and its importance to the tenure process has long been a controversial topic. Some argue that it leads to the suppression of unpopular or new ideas with which conservative editorial boards may not agree. Others believe that requiring so many librarians to publish dilutes the literature and results in the proliferation of mediocre publishing outlets whose real purpose is to provide a forum for those who need peer-reviewed publication credit rather than to contribute to the advancement of library research. As Philadelphia University Library Director Steven Bell comments: "I have never had a position where I had to write because of tenure requirements. I wish none of us had to. In my opinion this has contributed to an overabundance of library publications . . . to provide an outlet for librarians caught in the publish or perish track—and the result is a great number of duplicative and not so great quality articles being added to the literature. I think the ONLY reason you should write/publish is because you have something you want to communicate and share with your colleagues or to express a new idea—not because you are forced to do so."

As things stand now, peer-reviewed publication remains a tenure requirement in many institutions. If it is required in yours, the best approach is to view this as an opportunity to give back to the profession by contributing your work to the library literature. Avoid falling into the trap of mediocrity by understanding publication in scholarly journals as integrally related to your own professional development and as a way to share with your peers what you know and what you have learned.

As another somewhat cynical survey respondent suggests: "I see way too much publication in library journals that is pure junk, apparently done just to get one's name in print. I regret that the tenure/promotion system has made that necessary. Very little of what is published in library journals is actually worth reading. So—and I know this is idealistic—wait until you have something to say that people really need to hear, write it simply, without jargon, be brief, [and] get to the point quickly. People are busy and don't have time for much reading." Do what you can to avoid being part of the dilution of the literature; make your writing count, and you will stand out among your peers. Reluctant academic authors can find some tips on getting started in table 7.1.

Table 7.1. Tips for Reluctant Academic Authors

If you are reluctant to tackle the process of academic writing by the prospect of writing for peer-reviewed publications, tr lowing methods to ease into the process:

- *Work with a coauthor.* Remember from chapter 6 the importance of networking and collaboration to the library literature, and find someone to work with you in creating a peer-reviewed piece. Work with another newer librarian in order to support each other, or find a previously published collaborator and benefit from his/her experience.

- *Find a mentor.* Here, again, the willingness of other librarians to share their knowledge and experience can be invaluable. Ask senior colleagues in your institution for advice on the publishing process and get their comments on your work.

- *Submit your work to newer journals.* Newer publications such as *portal* (discussed later in this chapter) support a more nurturing peer-review process and sponsor their own mentoring programs.

- *Tackle simpler projects.* Survey articles, literature reviews, and those reporting on programs you have successfully instituted in your library can be easier to write and research than full-blown research articles.

- *Investigate related opportunities.* Some institutions' tenure committees may look equally favorably on conference poster sessions and other related activities as on peer-reviewed publication. Find out the requirements in your institution and diversify your professional efforts.

Peer-reviewed publication is also important because it helps librarians retain status in an academic environment. Libraries that institute peer-review requirements demonstrate that their faculty librarians are held to the same standards as faculty in other departments, and universities find it easier to compare (and compensate) librarians' contributions when they are also contributing to the academic literature. University of Toledo Assistant Dean for Library Systems Corey Seeman explains that: "In the academic environment, libraries with faculty status need to keep writing and presenting to anchor their role as a member of the campus academic community." Our peer-reviewed literature is part of what makes us both a profession and an academic discipline, and our research and the theories that stem from that research are what provide the foundation of librarianship itself.

There are personal rewards that accrue from academic publication as well. Publishing an article that you know has met the approval of an expert editor (or panel of editors) in your field can help you feel empowered in your own research and your own profession. It provides an outside validation of your work and can encourage you to make further contributions. It provides an opportunity for you to present your research to a community of your peers. The peer-review process itself allows you to have your work read and critiqued by experts in the field whose advice can help you make your piece—or your next piece—even stronger.

Publication allows you to contribute to your own professional development by researching, learning, and developing your own philosophies on topics of professional interest. Peggy Johnson notes: "Librarians with tenure track appointments may feel the most pressure to publish if this is one criterion for obtaining tenure and promotion. This external pressure can obscure a more compelling reason—the continuing need for professional growth. Writing effectively requires learning as much as possible about the issue being addressed and giving it intense consideration. This type of reflection on library issues is an essential characteristic of a professional librarian."[1]

The process of creating academic writing also provides you with an empathy for and greater ability to serve students and faculty engaged in similar research in your own institution. Corey Seeman continues: "As librarians, we help people find material they are looking for as it relates to their interest, assignments, or research. To better assist our patrons, we need to have traveled that path ourselves and do the research and understand the process. Research and publication helps move the profession forward, but it also helps us become better librarians." Academic research and publication helps integrate librarians into the life of the academy.

In response to librarians' concerns about peer-reviewed literature, newer journals are emerging that attempt to modify the process into something more nurturing for potential authors. Johns Hopkins University Press, for example, has since 2001 published *portal: Libraries and the Academy,* a quarterly online refereed journal focusing on librarianship and higher education. Editors at this journal have established an author mentoring system, which aims to help librarians work their research into publishable articles—whether for *portal* or for another publication. As they state in their author guidelines:

Major journals in most disciplines pride themselves on their high rejection rates, rationalizing that a high rejection rate signifies a strong commitment to and compelling evidence of quality. Nothing could be more wasteful of the scarce resources for library research than to replicate a system that encourages authors to create a finished product that is judged and summarily rejected.

By contrast, *portal* board, mentors, and editors are committed to help authors from the moment they decide to engage in research to the moment when they elect to submit the finished product either to *portal* or to some other journal. We foster a supportive and confidential environment for authors. Mentors are available to consult with authors about topic identification and selection, about issues around statistical sampling and survey design, and about crafting the article itself. We believe that early intervention enables aspiring authors to complete strong projects that are likely to be accepted for publication by an independent set of referees.[2]

Such efforts may help newer authors get started in peer-reviewed publication and bear watching as the peer-review process continues to be discussed and criticized. (For more on *portal,* see the interview with managing editor Gloriana St. Clair in appendix B.)

Other journal publishers have taken advantage of the online medium and its ability to allow them to streamline the publication process after acceptance of an article, allowing you to track your submissions and either check their status online or receive e-mail alerts at certain points along the way. Elsevier, for example, maintains an online author gateway at http://authors.elsevier.com, at which authors can sign up to track their papers' progress, locate author guidelines, and so on. (Information on their library science journals can be found under the "Social and Behavioral Sciences" category; for more on journals' adaptation to the electronic environment, see chapter 11.)

Because of the length of the publication process for many peer-reviewed journals, such tracking systems can be helpful at points when you feel certain your paper must have gotten misplaced somewhere along the way. Extra features such as online tracking may help you decide between two comparable outlets when picking where to submit your piece.

Many librarians, however, refuse to submit their work to large publishers such as Elsevier as a form of symbolic protest against excessive journal price increases and copyright issues, preferring to work with smaller, more affordable, and friendlier publishers. *portal* itself emerged as an alternative to the *Journal of Academic Librarianship* after the latter was acquired by Elsevier in the late 1990s. You will need to balance such philosophical considerations against the potential audience for your work and the relative prestige of particular journals when deciding on an appropriate outlet for your writing.

Research Articles

Research articles in peer-reviewed journals generally follow a similar format and take a similar tone. You may first be required to provide a short abstract (or synopsis) of your work and supply relevant keywords for publication with the article. In some cases, the journal editor(s) may create these for you. This requirement will be outlined in the publication's guidelines or will be explained as you embark on the publishing process. Realize that the abstract is often used in journal indexes and/or posted at a publisher's Web page. Make it descriptive enough that readers can ascertain the gist of your article and see if they wish to track it down and read the full text, and include appropriate keywords for indexing. Your ability to summarize your own work succinctly will come in handy throughout your career—in queries, in marketing copy, in summaries on your own Web site—and will also help you clarify your own thoughts and purpose in writing an article.

Following the abstract, you will then wish to provide an introduction and include a problem statement (or statement of purpose) succinctly explaining the issue you are researching and the question(s) you intend to answer. This establishes the need for your article and lets readers ascertain whether the later sections of your work answer the questions you intended to address. This is one of the most important parts of any academic paper; reviewers will judge your work largely on whether it answers your problem statement, and readers will look to this statement merely to find out what your article is about.

Many journals will then request that you include a review of the existing literature on your subject showing how others have approached the topic and providing a background for your newer research. Here, provide a summary of the major schools of thought on the issue and of any specific research you intend to challenge or extend with your own. The literature review both shows that you have done your homework and helps give your readers the background necessary to understand your own research.

This section leads into a description of your research methodology. This section should be sufficiently detailed so that readers could duplicate your research, if desired, and should explain why you chose this

Table 7.2. Suggested Research Methods Guides

Busha, Charles H., and Stephen P. Harter, eds. *Research Methods in Librarianship: Techniques and Interpretations.* New York: Academic Press, 1980.

Creswell, John W. *Research Design: Qualitative, Quantitative, and Mixed Methods Approaches.* 2nd ed. Thousand Oaks, Calif.: Sage, 2003.

Glazier, Jack D., and Ronald R. Powell. *Qualitative Research in Information Management.* Englewood, Colo.: Libraries Unlimited, 1992.

Gorman, G.E., and Peter Clayton. *Qualitative Research for the Information Professional: A Practical Handbook.* London: Library Association Publishing, 1997.

Leedy, Paul D., and Jeanne Ellis Ormrod. *Practical Research: Planning and Design.* 7th ed. Upper Saddle River, N.J.: Prentice-Hall, Inc., 2001.

Powell, Ronald R. *Basic Research Methods for Librarians.* 3rd ed. Greenwich, Conn.: Ablex Publishing Corp., 1997.

Slater, Margaret, ed. *Research Methods in Library and Information Studies.* London: The Library Association, 1990.

Sproull, Natalie L. *Handbook of Research Methods: A Guide for Practitioners and Students in the Social Sciences.* 2nd ed. Metuchen, N.J.: Scarecrow Press, 1995.

Vaughan, Liwen. *Statistical Methods for the Information Professional: A Practical, Painless Approach to Understanding, Using, and Interpreting Statistics.* Medford, N.J.: Information Today, Inc., 2001.

---

particular methodology to deal with the question(s) brought out by your problem statement. Following this, you will show how you collected your data—again, providing sufficient detail on the process.

The next, and most interesting, section of your article will provide an analysis of the data you collected during the research process. Here, you will analyze your data and show how the results answer the questions created by your problem statement. Do not simply summarize your results, but spend some time doing your analysis and showing how the data collected apply to the questions you raised earlier.

Lastly, provide your conclusions (which must derive directly from the results of your data). Explain the implications of your research to the field and to the problem you are addressing. Delineate any flaws you might have noticed in your own research and provide specific recommendations for further research on the subject. End with a list of references in the specific style and format favored by your journal.

You will also need to include any charts, tables, graphs, or other supporting material for your article. Each journal will have specific guidelines on formatting such material; some will prefer to receive it electronically. Be sure to include only the supporting material that is necessary to illustrate your points.

The previous paragraphs of course just summarize the elements of a typical research article; consult library research methods guides such as those in table 7.2 for detailed descriptions of each step in the process and instructions on effective data collection and analysis. Also consult journal guidelines and read prior issues to get an idea of the coverage of a particular publication.

Research in the library environment helps to provide data to aid librarians in their decision making and to provide evidence underpinning professional theories and beliefs. Librarians undertake professional research to support a goal, answer a particular question, provide a recommendation, or determine a direction for innovation. If your objective is unclear from the beginning, your research will lack focus and it will be difficult to compose an article on your subject. Remember also that the quality of your research is one of the most important factors in academic writing. Ensure that your research meets professional standards before even beginning to write your article and that your methodology is sufficiently robust.

Other types of academic articles include literature reviews, which survey and discuss the relevant scholarly literature on a specific topic, and theoretical articles, which address philosophical issues of importance to the profession. Consult a journal's guidelines and past issues to see which of these types of articles it is likely to publish before submitting your work. Realize that articles such as literature reviews do not just summarize the literature on a subject; they critically discuss its findings, strengths, and weaknesses.

Once you have submitted an article to a journal, it enters the peer-review process described in the previous section. If it is accepted for publication, either as originally submitted or after revision to meet reviewers' suggestions, it then enters the publishing process. This can be quite lengthy at some journals. Your article will be edited for content and style as well as copyedited, and then proofs will generally be sent to you for your approval (generally four to eight weeks after acceptance). Once the copy is approved as it will be published, the article enters the queue for publication, which, depending on the journal's backlog and publication schedule, can take anywhere from three months to over a year.

At some point in this process, the journal will send you a copyright release form or contract to sign. Read this carefully. Many academic publications will ask for all rights to your work and forbid you even from using your own article in a class or posting it on your own Web site. Be sure that you understand and can agree to whatever you are signing, including clauses on electronic rights, copyright, payment, and the due date of your article. (For more on contracts, see chapter 12.)

As always, be sure to investigate thoroughly the types of articles a scholarly journal publishes before submitting your proposal or manuscript. A common mistake among academic librarians is submitting their work only to the most well-known outlets without considering the appropriateness of those publications for their particular article, and the most common reason for rejection is inappropriateness of the outlet for a particular work. At the very least, check journals' mastheads for their statement of intent to see the types of articles they wish to publish, then look for guidelines and read past articles to familiarize yourself with their outlook, topics, and tone.

Research Funding, Support, and Awards

You may be more readily able to find sources of funding for academic research leading to publication than for other types of publishing activities. Realize, though, that the process of applying for research funding can be long and arduous, and that funding bodies may have particular requirements both for publication and for the research process itself. Balance these constraints against your needs. Such funding or awards may be the only remuneration you receive from academic publishing; many journals pay only in "author copies" of the issue in which your work appears. The sentiment here is that publication in an esteemed journal is reward in itself, or that its assistance toward achieving tenure or promotion outweighs any possible monetary compensation.

Several associations and endowments also present awards for outstanding original research in the profession, which are a coup not only because of their value as monetary rewards, but as significant professional achievements to add to your c.v. or promotion folder. Many awards do allow self-nominations, so if you have done significant research that you believe worthy of professional recognition, do not be shy about putting your work forward.

Such awards are not available only for those who have published in the field for years. LITA, for example, funds an annual student writing award for the best unpublished manuscript on libraries and information technology; the winner (who must be currently enrolled in an accredited graduate LIS program) receives $1,000, and his or her article is

Writers Support Committee
org/nmrt/

Association of Research Libraries (ARL)
http://www.arl.org

IFLA Library and Information Science Journals Section
http://www.ifla.org/VII/s45/slisj.htm

Library History Round Table (ALA)
http://www.spertus.edu/library-history/

Library Research Round Table (ALA)
http://www.ala.org/lrrt/

---

published in LITA's refereed *Information Technology and Libraries*. LAMA sponsors a similar writing award for currently enrolled students, publishing the winning article on a LAMA-specified topic in *Library Administration & Management* and providing $1,000 in funding for the winner to attend the annual ALA conference. Realize that such opportunities exist to promote the importance of research and publication to newer librarians, and, as a newer or potential librarian, be on the lookout for any such chance to promote your own writing and get it out to a wider audience.

Be on the lookout also for professional development grants from your state, your institution, and from associations. These are more likely to be awarded to those with a previous record of publication. (For more on grants, see chapter 1.) Search for grant opportunities on an association's Web site or keep an eye out for their announcement in association newsletters and journals.

Always investigate any research support and funding your institution makes available. Some provide the opportunity for sabbaticals or release time for research to faculty, including librarians. This uninterrupted time to complete a research project can be invaluable. Others may be willing to fund original research in librarianship, especially if it is likely to lead to publication in a prestigious peer-reviewed journal. Realize, however, that faculty from other disciplines will be less likely to be familiar with the purpose and usefulness of library research. Librarians pursuing support and funding inside of their own institutions may face an increased need to explain and defend their research. In most cases, the people who decide on the recipients of grants and awards will be nonlibrary faculty.

More experienced colleagues inside your institution may be willing to serve as official or unofficial mentors, or as collaborators, as you undertake your publishing efforts. They can suggest potential topics, read over drafts, help structure your research, and suggest which outlets may be more highly regarded by tenure committees in your particular institution.

As California State University, Long Beach Librarian Joy Thomas suggests: "Get trusted colleagues to review your work critically before you submit it. I've done that; it helped clarify my thoughts and I've never written anything that wasn't ultimately published somewhere." Academic research and publication helps make you part of the "invisible college" of colleagues that forms the backbone of the literature, and, at its best, this atmosphere can foster collaboration and cooperation among professional peers. Having others comment on your work also helps prepare you for the peer-review process, in a perhaps more congenial atmosphere. Some journals actively encourage this kind of "pre-print" circulation of articles as a method of receiving stronger works, and some academic institutions formalize this process by supporting critique groups for publishing faculty.

You may also consider registering your research projects with a database such as Emerald's Research Register, available online at http://gessler.emeraldinsight.com/vl=400154/cl=37/nw=1/rpsv/research register/lis.htm. This allows you to share pre-publication results, locate coauthors, view others' research, and get feedback on your own research.

Above all, do not let the prospect of academic publishing intimidate or silence you. Take the time to find the support you need and get your work out there; add your voice to the ongoing professional conversation. Academic publishing connects you to the larger community of both researchers and practitioners. As Mary Frank Fox writes: "Writing and publishing are not simply responsibilities; they constitute a great opportunity. They allow one to participate in, contribute to, and receive recognition from the discipline."[3] Look at publishing as your opportunity to join in.

Notes

1.   Peggy Johnson, "Writing for Publication," *Technicalities* 17, no. 2 (February 1997): 9.
2.   Susan K. Martin and Charles B. Lowry, "Guidelines for Contributors—*portal: Libraries and the Academy,*" 2001-2002, http://www.press.jhu.edu/press/journals/pla/information/guidelines.html (6 July 2002).
3.   Mary Frank Fox, *Scholarly Writing and Publishing: Issues, Problems, and Solutions* (Boulder, Colo.: Westview Press, 1985): 14.

Chapter 8
Related Opportunities

Once you have gotten your feet wet with your first publishing efforts in the library field, you may wish also to pursue writing for more general outlets. Writing for other audiences provides the advantage of getting your ideas out to a wider group and may in time prove more lucrative than your trade publishing activities. Articles relating to librarianship or on a variety of causes and topics near and dear to the library profession (such as intellectual freedom, copyright, research, authorship, or the Internet) often appear in general publications, and information professionals can offer a unique perspective on these issues.

Beyond writing for other outlets, take some time to investigate the variety of additional writing-related opportunities the profession itself offers. In addition to publishing books and articles in library literature, you can consider taking up book reviewing, writing conference reports, penning letters to the editor, writing for electronic newsletters, and presenting papers and poster sessions at association meetings. Taking advantage of these opportunities can be a great way to begin your career in library publication by creating shorter, less intimidating pieces that allow you to build your confidence and effectiveness as a writer.

Any writing you do, in whatever venue or medium, allows you to contribute to the profession or to the profession's image. Shorter or more informal pieces in library literature add your voice to the ongoing conversation about our profession, its foundations, and where it is headed, while your contributions to the general press or to the literature of other disciplines allow interaction between different fields and shows others the impact of the information profession. The sections in this chapter describe a number of related writing opportunities and show the broad range of our professional communication.

You may also wish to contribute to the profession via nonwritten forms of communication such as speaking, presenting, or preparing poster sessions or hosting talk tables at local workshops or at professional conferences. All of these forms of professional communication interact, and your success as a presenter will influence your skill and success as a writer.

Speaking and Presenting

As you become more well-known as a writer in the library field, you will find that your expertise makes you in demand as a speaker and presenter as well. This is especially true if you begin to specialize in a particular subject area, as those searching for speakers have an extensive and consistent body of work to draw upon in learning your positions and reviewing your research. Conference organizers and others hunting for speakers often find candidates by perusing the library literature to locate experts on a particular topic. It is also possible that an article or book you have written may stick in their mind when it is time to find a presenter.

As Sally Decker Smith, head of adult services at the Indian Trails Public Library District, notes of her experience as a regular columnist for the Illinois Library Association's newsletter: "I am becoming well-known in Illinois, and am asked to speak at library events all over the place on occasion. My goal is to make enough money speaking and writing in retirement that I can afford to keep myself supplied with chocolate!"

Speaking engagements growing out of your published work can help you make contacts and find ideas for additional articles, creating a positive feedback cycle that can greatly benefit your career. Presenting at association meetings, for example, gives you the opportunity to network with your peers and to attend other workshops and sessions. These opportunities can spark your creativity and allow you to identify potential collaborators, article topics, or additional outlets for your work. Chicago Library System's Theresa A. Ross Embrey shares: "A recent article on a hot topic that I wrote has led to the scheduling of a couple of nonlocal speaking engagements. The resulting travel has been enlightening and exhilarating. It has given me more to write about."

Stay alert to these networking opportunities whenever and wherever you serve as a presenter. If attendees speak with you or e-mail comments after your presentation, for example, find out more about what they are working on—you never know if a potential editor or collaborator may be sitting in your audience. Feedback you receive from your presentations can also let you know if you have a useful and publishable idea. Philadelphia University Library Director Steven Bell explains: "I test many ideas by delivering them at conferences—if they go well, I find it is much easier to turn them into articles." Speaking requires different skills than does writing, but your actual content may be quite similar. You are in either case organizing your thoughts around a topic (which may be assigned by the conference organizers or group), researching this topic, and presenting your conclusions in a logical order.

Given this similarity in content and requirements, you may be able later to publish the papers that you have presented at library conferences. Although you will often need to rework your presentation to make it appropriate for written publication, you will already have done the bulk of the necessary research and work in putting it together. More scholarly conferences may publish your paper as a matter of course in their conference proceedings. This provides you with both a speaking and a writing credit from a single engagement, and is one factor to consider in deciding whether to accept an offer to speak.

Keep in mind that editors also attend conferences, either as vendors or in their "day job" capacity as working librarians. Conference presenters are often later contacted by editors asking them to expand or modify their presentation for publication—you never know who might be in your audience! Tracy Englert, catalog librarian at the University of Southern Mississippi, shares her experience: "After a poster session with another librarian at ALA Annual in Atlanta this year (2002), I received a letter from the editor for *Technical Services Quarterly* to see if I'd be interested in turning the poster session into an article. I also received an e-mail from [the] SELA (Southeastern Library Association [journal]) editor about this possibility."

You may also be able to gain new ideas for your writing through interaction with your audiences. If your presentations are followed by question-and-answer sessions, for example, pay attention to the types of questions people ask. These may be intriguing questions they have been unable to find answers to in the existing literature, questions that you can answer briefly in person but then expand on in your later work.

This lets you fill in the gap for them (and for others) and creates a made-to-order publishing opportunity—you already know that interest exists in your topic. Make note of any informal conversations you have with attendees after the session and be alert to ideas that may grow out of these discussions.

As an added bonus, presenting at association conferences provides you with the opportunity to go to meetings you may otherwise never have been able to attend. Conference fees are often waived for presenters, and, as you become more well-known, associations will be more willing to reimburse your travel and expenses and to compensate you for your time and effort. (If fees and expenses are not waived, consider whether you wish to pay to attend, or see if your home institution will be more willing to fund your attendance if you are serving as a presenter. Note that ALA and other large associations may neither compensate nor waive conference costs for member panel presenters.) Since your presentation or workshop fills only one conference time slot, take the chance to participate in additional sessions, exhibits, and other conference-related opportunities.

Speaking at library-related events also gives you an opportunity to market yourself and your work. (See chapter 10 for more on marketing.) Include information on your published writing in your handouts and your speaker biography. If you have written a book, see if your publisher will provide you with flyers or other publicity materials to hand out at your presentations; be sure that these include an easy-to-mail order form, or at least full ordering information for the title. If your publisher does not provide flyers, make up your own brochure and hand out copies to attendees. The mere act of speaking and having your name listed in conference materials will also assist you in building name recognition for yourself and your work, especially if you make a habit of speaking and writing on similar topics.

Presenting at professional conferences can be an alternate way of impressing tenure and promotion committees, if you feel more comfortable as a speaker than as a writer. It serves as an alternate method of professional communication, can help build your confidence and expertise on a subject, and can help provide you with material you can later publish once you are more comfortable with the prospect of writing for an academic journal.

Related Library Writing Opportunities

In addition to articles and books, there are a number of related opportunities that allow you to enter the library publication process gradually before beginning to tackle larger projects, or to contribute shorter pieces in between writing longer works.

Brief Is Better

Writing book and electronic resource reviews, for example, allows you to create short, focused pieces while also contributing to the library literature. Because collection development is such a vital part of any thriving library, reviews serve an important purpose. Reviewers make an invaluable contribution to the profession. As David Scott, reference and ILL librarian at Ferris State University, notes: "A product may or may not get purchased based upon what I write. That's a fairly large responsibility, one we need to have respect for." Further, since library journals often review titles that receive less attention in the general media, you may have the opportunity to discover and read less-publicized but interesting works that you would not otherwise have encountered.

One survey respondent suggests that newer writers "start small. Volunteer to review books, magazines, media, and Web sites. (If nothing else, reviewing teaches you how to write concisely!)" Although reviewing generally does not pay, you usually get to keep the item being reviewed and also have the opportunity to build name recognition and material for your c.v. through signed reviews. Reviewing also provides a convenient focus in the book or item being reviewed for those who have trouble breaking their ideas into publishable form or who have difficulty finding article topics.

Reviewing may seem simple on the surface. Condensing a work down to a short evaluative description, however, can be more difficult than most librarians anticipate; realize that magazines such as *Library Journal* that publish a large number of reviews in each issue limit book reviewers to a mere 150-200 words per review. (Use the "word count" feature in your word processor to avoid exceeding your limit.) Reviewing, therefore, presents an invaluable opportunity to learn to write clearly and concisely. Review style differs from journal to journal; some may allow several-page reviews while others publish only brief evaluations. These guidelines will be provided when you begin reviewing for a publication; also familiarize yourself with the journal's style by reading a number of published reviews before applying to become a reviewer.

Watch for calls for reviewers in the various library publications you read and the review sources you use in your own collection development activities. Find these calls in the book review section itself, or they may be posted on topical e-mail lists as well. When you apply to review for a publication, most journals will require you to submit a query, your résumé, and a sample review or two so that they can evaluate your potential as a reviewer. They will also ask for a list of subject areas in which you prefer to review, although you should not count on receiving only items in your preferred subject area. To gain experience, you can even start writing book reviews for your own library's newsletter or inquire about writing them for your local newspaper.

Your main duty as a reviewer is to take the time to be fair to the book or other resource, providing both a useful analysis for other librarians and a fair shake to the author. When reviewing a book, do not cheat—read the whole title and write your own review before reading others' (whether in the library literature or in other sources such as Amazon.com). Be fair, remembering that someday, someone may be reviewing your work! Do not, however, feel constrained to always write a positive review. Librarians need to know the books to avoid adding to the collection and the drawbacks of certain items. Add your critical perspective rather than just summarizing the title. Do justice to the work itself, even if you are not usually a fan of the particular genre or subject you are assigned. Who knows, you may expand your own horizons and find that a title unexpectedly catches your interest.

Review outlets in the library field include the major publications such as *Library Journal, School Library Journal, VOYA, CHOICE, Booklist,* and *Reference Reviews.* Many other journals include a review or two in each issue; again, the best way to become familiar with these publications is to make a habit of regularly reading or browsing them. Online newsletters and journals such as *Free Pint* and *Technology Electronic Reviews* also often review books and other resources. Rather than assigning specific titles to review, though, more informal publications such as e-newsletters may ask you to pick your own title to review from a list of items they have available, or to suggest a particular book you think might be appropriate for review and then obtain your own copy of the item. They are also more likely to review professional materials than to cover general titles.

Look for opportunities to review Web sites and electronic resources as well. Publications such as *Reference Reviews* cover a large number of databases and Web sites, and *Library Journal's* "Web-

Watch" column is an example of an outlet always seeking reviewers. (*LJ* regularly posts a call for contributors in the WebWatch column itself, seeking contributors willing to create a full column that selects and annotates the most useful Web sites on a particular topic.) Query for such column opportunities just as you would for a more general article, and note that publishers of these longer collections of reviews do often pay at least a minimal stipend.

You may be more marketable as a contributor for these longer columns if you have previous reviewing experience. Although you are generally not compensated as an occasional reviewer for a publication, after you have built up your reputation you may in time be asked to take on additional paid responsibilities such as a regular review column, or to contribute to the journal by writing an article in your review area.

Beyond reviewing, you will find a number of other opportunities to publish brief and practical content in the library literature. A simple way to begin is by expressing your opinion on others' work via letters to the editor. Most journals have a section soliciting reader feedback, much of which is reprinted in the publication. Your signed letter, especially if accompanied by an e-mail address, can lead others to contact you to express their agreement or disagreement with your position— expanding your network of correspondents and again increasing your name recognition among your peers. Yes, "anyone" can write a letter to the editor—but not all letters are published, and those of substance will be read and recognized. Treat letter writing seriously and make sure that your letters exhibit the same quality as your other writing.

While you may not tend to think of letters as a form of publication, any writing that appears in the official literature both contributes to the profession and helps make your views known. Everyone's viewpoint is valuable, and letters can be a good way for newer librarians to participate in the literature and gain confidence in expressing their opinions without the pressures of creating a longer piece under deadline. Every time you sit down with a current journal, make note of articles that particularly strike you and think of opinions on those articles that you might wish to share with the author and with your peers.

Other opportunities present themselves in the form of short conference reports in association newsletters and related publications. At each conference, associations and committees solicit volunteers to write up reports of what went on in particular programs, conference sessions, and meetings. These reports appear in publications such as ALA's *Cognotes* and in newsletters of association subgroups, which are often mailed to each member of the group or larger association.

Since large conferences such as ALA Annual contain a plethora of programs, associations need a number of conference reporters to ensure the widest possible coverage. Like book reviewing, conference reporting generally does not pay but provides an easy chance to get your name in front of a wide audience and to practice writing concisely and practically. Conference reports are short, descriptive accounts of what went on at a session or meeting; you will wish to touch on the highlights of the program, give an idea of what was presented or discussed, and give an idea of the quality of the event. Be sure to take detailed notes at the sessions you are reporting on and to report accurately on presenters' names and affiliations.

Calls for conference reporters are often posted on the e-mail lists sponsored by associations and subgroups and/or on the association's Web site. Print association newsletters and magazines may include such calls some time before a conference is scheduled—another reason to keep current with your professional reading.

Keep current with your online reading as well. Writing for electronic newsletters or for library-related Web sites is another good way to get started in less-formal forms of library publication. (For more on publishing in the electronic environment, see chapter 11.) Sites and online newsletters maintained by librarians are always seeking content. Priscilla Shontz's LISCareer.com Web site, for example (http://www.liscareer.com/contact.htm), seeks short career advice pieces, as does Lisjobs.com's *Info Career Trends* newsletter (http://www.lisjobs.com/newsletter/). Judith Siess, president of Information Bridges International, Inc., suggests: "Keep at it. Try some of the small newsletters—especially the online ones. They are always looking for material."

More informal online publications do fill a niche in the library literature, providing outlets for different types of articles and points of view that are not necessarily found in traditional print publications. Writing for a more informal, non-peer-reviewed electronic site or newsletter, further, can be more immediately gratifying than writing for a print publication, as the turnaround time is often faster and communication with your editor will likely take place exclusively via e-mail, obviating the need to wait for comments and manuscripts to arrive in the mail.

While none of these opportunities "counts" as peer-reviewed publication and will be less impressive in the eyes of most tenure committees, contributing to the profession in this way provides broader advantages. These range from the name recognition you gain from any publication to valuable practice in composing a piece of professional writing. Outside of academic environments, any publication is generally looked on favorably, especially if it brings recognition to your institution.

Editorial Review

You might also consider being willing to serve as a volunteer on an editorial review board. Journals occasionally post calls for review board members, just as they post calls for contributors. Your responsibilities as an editorial board member will include the willingness to review articles in your area of expertise and to make recommendations as to whether they are publishable in the journal. The journal will provide you with guidelines for manuscript evaluation, which you should follow as carefully as you would follow a publication's author guidelines when composing your own work.

You will also be called upon to comment on manuscripts, provide substantive criticism, and make suggestions as to any necessary revisions. Understand from the outset the time commitment necessary. The journal's editor should be able to give you an idea of the average number of manuscripts you will be asked to evaluate annually.

You will be more likely to be selected (or asked to serve) as an editorial board member once you have some published pieces to your credit. You should also have demonstrable expertise in the journal's main subject area.

While you will not typically be monetarily compensated for such work, it will be a coup for your résumé and may count favorably in the eyes of a tenure/promotion committee if you are working in an academic environment. You are also making a contribution to the library literature. Reviewers perform an invaluable service as gatekeepers, passing through work that is suitable for publication and helping strengthen articles in order that they can be published. Further, reading others' writing with a critical eye can help strengthen your own work—you can see firsthand the difference between publishable and unpublishable manuscripts and learn what makes a stronger piece of writing. You also will get the opportunity to keep up to date by viewing articles in the field before anyone else!

Opportunities Outside the Library Literature

Be alert also for opportunities to publish your work outside what is traditionally thought of as "the library literature." Librarianship is necessarily an interdisciplinary profession, and we have much to contribute both to other fields and to the general literature.

Publishing in other fields unrelated to librarianship allows us to expand our audience. As Jay H. Bernstein, executive director of the Library of Social Science Book Exhibits, suggests: "You may want to publish outside the purely library-oriented literature. [If] you are a chemistry librarian you may want to send something to a chemistry journal. This would make your work more accessible to specialists in that field, where library journals wouldn't get their things indexed there." You will find a new group of readers and a new opportunity to extend your name recognition outside of the library profession.

You can also look at publishing for outside journals as an opportunity to inform nonlibrarians about issues important to the profession—and about what we do! One survey respondent, Massachusetts Board of Library Commissioners Consultant, Library Services to the Unserved Shelley Quezada, states: "We should be looking to publish as much as possible 'outside' of library literature as well. We have a big hurdle to jump in reaching the public who do not read library literature."

There are a number of fields related to librarianship that could also benefit from the perspective of experienced librarians. Philadelphia University Library Director Steven Bell says, "I would encourage librarians to think broadly about publishing and not limit themselves to the library literature. We have some amazing ideas that we can contribute to the literature of professions that are peripheral to our own. For example, academic librarians could be contributing much more to the literature of higher education, pedagogy, teaching/learning, and educational technology."

You can seek to publish the results of research in your area of specialization, whether or not these are at all specific to librarianship, and whether or not you choose to submit this research to journals in the field. Contribution to the peer-reviewed literature of other disciplines can help librarians advance in a tenure-track environment and thrive in an academic atmosphere. While you may have obstacles to overcome among other librarians who have difficulty recognizing the merits of writing for other audiences, take the opportunity to educate your peers. Kenneth E. Carpenter writes that "librarians need to foster outstanding accomplishments among all kinds of librarians. It goes, of course, almost without saying that a librarian's contribution to the literature of a humanistic discipline should not be devalued on the grounds that it is not about library issues."[1]

Realize that whenever you are writing for a nonlibrary audience, you will need to minimize your use of library jargon. You cannot assume the same commonality of background as when you are writing exclusively for other information professionals. Therefore, publishing for a general audience gives you the opportunity to try a completely different style of writing, and the practice can help bring clarity to your future professional writing as well.

Notes

1.   Kenneth E. Carpenter, "The Librarian-Scholar," *Journal of Academic Librarianship* 23, no. 5 (September 1997): 400.

Chapter 9
Writing a Book

Before beginning the process of creating a book proposal and submitting it to publishers, be very confident that you are able and willing to make the commitment to complete the entire manuscript. Writing a book, although similar to other professional writing, requires a higher level of dedication. It requires you to develop some unique skills. It will consume your free time and your thoughts for at least six months to a year (or sometimes considerably longer!), and you will need to spend much of that time ensuring that the book maintains a coherent argument throughout and that chapters and sections flow together naturally.

Your first step is to make sure that you have an idea that is extensive enough to warrant a whole book. Consider your topic carefully and picture the chapters and content you plan on including—if you are unable to create a mental image of an entire book, then start planning an article query instead. If this is your first foray into professional writing, you will likely wish to start by writing shorter pieces rather than tackling an extensive book project. Publishing articles first also gives you a body of work to draw upon. When you approach publishing houses with an idea for a longer work, your previously published writing can show them that you have developed some expertise in the field and give them an idea of your writing style and abilities.

Also realize that first-time book authors can tend to miscalculate the effort and time that will be needed to complete an entire manuscript. One survey respondent notes that "the sheer size of a book project can be overwhelming, and it's hard to maintain momentum." Another respondent concurs, saying that "writing a book was much harder [than publishing an article], because it lasted so much longer. I had no 'life' during the process."

Make sure to pick a topic that can sustain your interest throughout this process and that your writing will not interfere unduly with your work and other responsibilities; most library authors lack the time or funding to take a sabbatical to write a book and must complete their manuscript while still holding down a full-time job. Go back to the section in chapter 1 on finding ideas, remembering that the best topics are those that you are passionate about. If they resonate with you, you will be better able to make them resonate with your readers. As William Germano points out: "It's sometimes hard to keep in mind that any book you write is a book you're writing for yourself. But it is surely true that if you don't believe in your book, nobody else will."[1] If you believe in your book, organize your time, and make writing a part of your daily routine, the process is less likely to take over your life.

These warnings are not intended to scare you away from the idea of publishing a book. Writing a monograph can be quite personally and professionally rewarding. Writing books rather than articles allows you the room to expand on your ideas and arguments and to undertake broader research projects, as well as to explore another style of writing. Seeing your name on the cover of your first title—or listed in your library's OPAC—is also a reward in itself! You should, however, be aware of the magnitude of the task you are undertaking and the commitment you are making before you decide to submit your idea to a publisher.

Some librarian authors even prefer the book writing process and the freedom it gives them to expand on their ideas. Jay H. Bernstein, the executive director of Library of Social Science Book Exhibits, explains: "Since journal articles can involve a great amount of work getting them published, you may want to consider writing a book instead. That way you could say what you really want to say and spend your energy writing the book rather than the endless back and forth work trying to satisfy journal editors and reviewers."

If you do decide to go ahead with your proposal, follow it as closely as possible while writing after it is accepted by an editor. While your research will of course uncover additional material and possible new directions in which to take your original ideas, and your manuscript will evolve as you write, do not make the mistake of ignoring what you originally proposed. Your work was accepted on the basis of your proposal, and it is unfair (and dangerous) to turn in something completely other than what the editor is expecting. For this reason, put a great deal of care into composing your initial proposal and ensure that it accurately reflects your intentions. (For more on proposal writing, see chapter 3.)

Lastly, realize that while general publishing houses now prefer that most proposal submissions come through literary agents, this is not necessary for smaller library presses. You will need to turn to an agent only if you at some point choose to write for a broader audience and submit your work to a larger, nonlibrary press.

Developing a Topic

The first step in the monograph publication process is to select a topic that can carry a whole book. As an aid in jump-starting this process, turn to the section in chapter 1 on finding ideas for your writing. Be alert to possible subjects throughout your daily work while creating shorter writing projects and doing your professional reading.

One of the best ways to develop a topic for your book is to revisit your previously published articles or presentations and see whether any contain ideas that could be fleshed out into a longer work. Look back and see if you have written shorter pieces where you ended up doing more research or had more to say than could be included comfortably in your article. If you were forced to leave good material out, this may be a sign that you have a topic that lends itself to a book-length treatment. Incorporate this previous research and writing in your search for a subject and in writing your book proposal.

Alternatively, you can test out your book idea by publishing articles on smaller aspects of your subject. This gives you both additional publishing credentials and allows you to gauge potential interest in a book on your topic. You can later draw on the research you do for these articles while writing the book.

You can also find ideas by noticing gaps in the existing monograph literature. If there is a topic you yourself have tried to research and you have been unable to locate existing titles, this may be an indication of a need for someone to write a book on the subject. Why not you? If you have been disappointed by existing titles or have noticed that books on a topic you are interested in take a different approach than what you would like, consider writing a complementary work that approaches a subject in a new way or incorporates different or newer information.

Make sure before beginning this process, however, that you have investigated the titles that seem to compete and avoid duplicating work that has already been done.

Look at existing series from the major library publishers when developing your topic. Would your idea fit into the "How to Do It" series from Neal-Schuman, for example, or the "Genreflecting" series from Libraries Unlimited? If your idea naturally falls into one of these series, you have an additional selling point when you approach a publisher, a marketing plus for your book when it comes out, and a template to follow when you are writing. Realize, however, that publishing as part of a series means that your manuscript must follow the series format in order to fit in with the other volumes; do not propose a title for an existing series if you would feel constrained by its format.

Once you have a topic in mind for your book, start by trying to write out the table of contents for the work you envision. See if your subject lends itself to logical divisions and if you have an idea on how you will fill each chapter. You may also try to create a more detailed outline, if this will help you picture how your idea will be transformed into an actual book. The work you do here will be useful, not only in envisioning your title but in composing the book proposal itself.

You can also consider serving as editor for an anthology or compilation, which at its most basic involves identifying contributors, coordinating submissions, and editing their work. Editing opportunities will be more likely to present themselves once you have already made a name for yourself in the library literature. And, while on the face of it, editing a collected work may seem easier than writing an entire monograph yourself, it is not always so simple. The work you do in selecting contributors, getting their agreement to participate, getting them to turn work in on time and to follow guidelines, persuading them to sign release forms in a timely manner, writing introductions, and making contributions fit into a single coherent volume may give you a new sympathy for journal editors.

Lastly, realize that as your reputation and list of publications grow, an editor may approach you directly to write for his/her press on a specific subject. If the topic interests you and you feel you could reasonably complete the project, go for it! You will know from the outset that you have the interest and support of your editor, and saying yes can also bring additional work your way in the future. If you have suggestions about or modifications to the original idea, by all means discuss these with the editor. He/She should welcome your input, and between the two of you, you should be able to work out a stronger subject.

Choosing a Publisher

Just as there are a multiplicity of outlets for your professional articles, you will also find a library press devoted to publishing nearly any type of professional monograph. Most common in the library field is the "how-to" book, which lives up to its name in providing solid, practical advice to working librarians on how to do anything from choosing a new automation system to managing library staff. How-to guides are published by a number of library presses, from ALA Editions to Neal-Schuman. ALA Editions and several other publishing houses also publish titles on many other topics, including general works on library history, on the profession itself, bibliographies and guidebooks, and on topics currently affecting the profession (such as copyright, censorship, and information literacy).

Scholarly presses provide an outlet for book-length academic research; you may consider these if you have published several research articles on a topic and have more to say than can reasonably be expressed in the limited space allowed in academic journals. As with academic articles, a title for a scholarly press will favorably impress tenure and promotion committees. Scholarly presses will have similar requirements for their authors as well—their proposal guidelines usually require authors to outline their research methodology, for example.

As you read in the professional literature, keep track of who is publishing the titles that you find most useful. Make a note of the style, tone, and format of different publishers. Sign up to be included on their mailing lists and to receive free catalogs of forthcoming publications, which will show you if they are publishing in topics similar to yours. You can generally do this through filling out an online form on each publisher's Web site, or can at least browse their online listings to find additional information on new titles. Also visit publishers' sites to find information on the types of manuscripts they are currently looking for, proposal guidelines, and information on which editor handles which subjects.

Ask your colleagues who have published about their experiences, both positive and negative, with their publishing houses and editors. If you have a mentor in your academic institution, get his/her viewpoint. Getting honest feedback on others' experiences is the most useful way to see what publishing with a particular house is truly like.

When you attend professional conferences, make a habit of stopping by the booths of the publishers you are considering. Look through their current titles; chat with the editors staffing the exhibit. Be sure,

Table 9.1. Selected Publishers in the Library Field

ALA Editions
50 E. Huron St.
Chicago, IL 60611
Phone: 800-545-2433, ext. 3244
Fax: 312-944-8741
http://www.ala.org/editions/

Information Today
143 Old Marlton Pike
Medford, NJ 08055-8750
Phone: 609-654-6500
Fax: 609-654-4309
http://books.infotoday.com

Facet Publishing
7 Ridgmount Street
London WC1E 7AE
Tel: +44 (0)20 7255 0590
Fax: +44 (0)20 7255 0591
http://www.facetpublishing.co.uk

Libraries Unlimited
88 Post Road West
Westport, CT 06881
Phone: 800-225-5800
Fax: 203-222-1205
http://www.lu.com

Greenwood Publishing Group
88 Post Road West, Box 5007
Westport, CT 06881
Phone: 203-226-3571
Fax: 203-750-9790
http://www.greenwood.com

· McFarland
Box 611
Jefferson, NC 28640
Phone: 336-246-4460
Fax: 336-246-5018
http://www.mcfarlandpub.com

Haworth Press
10 Alice St.
Binghamton, NY 13904
Phone: 1-800-429-6784
Fax: 1-800-895-0582
http://www.haworthpressinc.com

Neal-Schuman
100 Varick St.
New York, NY 10013
Phone: 212-925-8650
Fax: 212-219-8916
http://www.neal-schuman.com

Highsmith Press
PO Box 800
Ft. Atkinson, WI 53538
Phone: 920-563-9571
Fax: 920-563-4801
http://www.hpress.highsmith.com

Scarecrow Press
4501 Forbes Blvd., Suite 200
Lanham, MD 20706
Phone: 301-459-3366
Fax: 301-429-5747
http://www.scarecrowpress.com

however, to keep your discussions with editors at these events brief and professional—these are long conferences, and they have a number of people to talk to.

Table 9.1 lists contact information for several major library presses. Keep in mind that most publishers will welcome written inquiries rather than phone calls, and that you should always address your correspondence to the correct and current acquisitions editor. (You may call to confirm an editor's information, but never to pitch your proposal unless invited to do so.) Editors' names are not listed in this table due to the rapid turnover in the book industry. Check publishers' Web sites for information on current editors and the types of manuscripts each handles. Many editors in the library field are former librarians who are familiar with the profession.

You will want to select the publishing house that is both most likely to publish your work and most likely to be able to work with you to properly promote it. If you are writing on library topics, realize that there are a limited number of publishers that specialize in the field—so there is no excuse for not doing your research on each before submitting your proposal! Choose a publisher that would reasonably consider a title on your topic—visit their Web site and look at their other titles to gauge the appropriateness of your proposal. Also consider how well various presses would be able to market your work. Does your topic reach their normal audience? Have you personally seen promotion for their other titles?

The Acceptance Process

After submitting a proposal, you will generally hear back from the publisher within a few weeks—although some presses may take as long as several months to respond. The length of your wait often depends on the size of the publishing house and on their existing backlog. If the publisher turns down the manuscript, they will generally send back a rejection letter in your SASE. If they wish to accept your proposal, they are more likely to phone or e-mail to discuss the details with you more personally.

If your proposal is rejected, dust yourself off and move on. Some publishers may give reasons for their rejection; use your own judgment as to the validity of their reasoning, modify your proposal as appropriate, and submit it to the next press on your list. (Be sure to change the proposal to adhere to that publisher's specific guidelines.) It may take multiple tries to find the appropriate press for your idea, or you may in the end find that you have misjudged the level of interest in your topic.

At some point you may need to determine that it is time to let this proposal go and to move on to new projects.

Publishers may also request that you make certain changes to your book proposal before they can consider your title for publication. Just as in the peer-review process, you need to decide whether these requested changes will strengthen your work and whether you wish to rework your proposal to meet a publisher's requirements.

Once an editor has accepted your proposal, he/she will discuss details, such as the expected delivery date and length of your manuscript, and make comments on areas he/she might wish to see fleshed out or included in the final manuscript. You will then receive a copy of the publisher's standard contract that you will need to sign and mail back. (For more detail on publishing contracts, see chapter 12.)

The Writing and Editing Process

The process of writing a book can consume your time and attention for months, if not for years. A little organization and determination, however, can go a long way toward easing this process and making your writing flow more smoothly. Set a schedule at the outset that will bring you forward to your deadline. If you are working with a coauthor, divide up the chapters right away so that you are both aware of your responsibilities and can set your individual timetables.

See chapter 5 for much more on writing and editing professional work. The process of writing a book, though, generally includes:

1. Researching your topic. Although this is the first step in the process (your research telling you whether your topic will fill a whole book), it also needs to continue throughout the entire writing and editing process. Ongoing research may bring to light new facts which will cause you to rewrite sections of your work. Newer material may emerge or be published as you are writing, and you need to be alert and aware of this possibility. It may help to organize your research, photocopies, and notes into folders by chapter. Keep a copy of your working table of contents handy to refer to during the research and writing process.

2. Outlining your work. Again, this may be more or less formal depending on your personal work style. But you will at some point need to straighten out what material goes where, the order of your chapters, and so on. Doing at least an initial outline before begin-

ning to write can help organize your thoughts and will make the
writing itself flow much more easily.

3. Writing the book. Keep each chapter in an individual computer
    file. Publishers will want your manuscript this way if you are sub-
    mitting it electronically, and this will also help you organize your
    chapters and your thoughts. If you have material that does not fit
    into the main flow of the writing, consider adding sidebars or ta-
    bles that contain this added information.

4. Editing your work. When you have finished writing, put the book
    aside for a while so that you can return to it with a fresh eye.

5. Rewriting the book. Your editing and continued research will
    likely reveal large sections of your work that need rewriting or re-
    working.

6. Editing again. Give it a final going-over to make sure everything
    flows smoothly, nothing is left out, and that this is your best work.

7. Preparing the manuscript. Make sure that your finished work ad-
    heres to the publisher's guidelines on format and style.

Additional steps may be needed, given the type of work you are
writing. At some point during the process, for example, you will need
to get permission for any reprints, graphics, or other such materials you
are including in your work. You may conduct a survey or interview
other librarians. Make sure all of this is done well in advance of your
deadline so that it can be incorporated naturally into your writing.

Many writers find it useful or less intimidating while writing to
view each chapter as a separate entity. Writing each chapter as a separate piece of work allows those who are used to working on articles or
other short pieces to ease into the process of writing a book. It can also
serve as a good organizing tool and can help you feel more comfortable
with writing chapters out of order. However, this technique requires a
good deal of rewriting and editing at the end to ensure that the chapters
logically flow together and that their content is not unduly repetitive.

While writing, keep track of the length of your manuscript and ensure that you do not dramatically exceed the number of words initially
agreed upon with your editor. If you are running over, start making
cuts—it is the rare manuscript that could not benefit from tightening
up. Realize that longer books cost publishers more to produce, and they
will not welcome excess pages they had not counted on receiving when
you initially discussed your project with your editor and signed your
publishing contract.

When you finish writing, put the book aside for some time before
going back to do your final rereading and editing of the manuscript.

Then it is time to get it ready to turn in to your editor. You will want to print or save the manuscript exactly as specified in your contract and in your publisher's guidelines. Most publishers will want double-spaced copy with minimal formatting; this they will add themselves.

If your contract, on the other hand, specifies camera-ready copy, you will be provided with very specific guidelines on laying out and formatting your text. Realize that the book will be produced from your layout, so be sure to follow guidelines exactly.

With the main body of your manuscript, also include any added material requested by the publisher, such as an "about the author" statement and photograph, a table of contents, an acknowledgments page, and so on. Include copies of all permissions you have received in a separate folder, as well as all reproductions or printouts of all art and illustrations. If the publisher has sent you an author questionnaire to complete (see chapter 10), this is also usually due with the final manuscript.

If you are submitting computer files with your printed copy, do not make changes to the files after you have printed out the work; these must be identical. Save each chapter as its own file, and keep backups of all your work. Your publisher will likely want art and screenshots in electronic format; include these as separate files as well. Label all files clearly and provide a list for the publisher explaining the contents of each.

The Publishing Process

After you turn in your manuscript, it can take anywhere from six months to a year before you are holding an actual copy of your published book. Be sure to do all you can to help keep this process on schedule. If the publisher sends you proofs to look at, get them back promptly. If you are indexing your own title, turn in the index on deadline.

It may take one to two months for your editor to get around to reading your manuscript once you send it in. Be patient; editors are busy people. The editor will then contact you with suggestions for changes in content and organization. Listen with an open mind and be prepared to accept some modifications; also be prepared to defend your content and work logically and calmly. This can be difficult, given that you have invested significant time and effort in creating your manuscript, but realize that your editor has had a great deal of experience in turning manuscripts into books. His/Her suggestions can help make your work stronger—and more saleable.

Once you have agreed on and made these broad content changes, your manuscript will be sent to a copy editor. (Copy editors are often freelancers and not direct employees of the publisher.) He/She will go over the work line by line with a fine-toothed comb to clear up any grammatical errors, spelling errors, typos, and so on. Some presses will send the copyedited manuscript with handwritten corrections for you to look over; others will skip this step, merely make the appropriate changes, and send you a typeset galley, or "proof," to look at some months later. This stage is your last chance to make changes to or spot errors in the manuscript, but you will not wish at this point to make major modifications. These will lead to the publisher needing to re-layout portions of the book and delay its publication.

At some point, the publisher will also likely send or e-mail a copy of the cover art for you to look at. Most publishing houses give authors little input into the look of their cover, but if you truly dislike the design, make your opinion known. Your book will be assigned an ISBN number and the look of the cover, including any endorsements or descriptions, will be finalized. The publisher will also set a price for the title, depending on factors such as its size, paperback or hardcover, its estimated market, and so on. Again, you will have little say here—trust the publisher's experience in this area.

When the proof is finished and the final copy of the book is typeset and laid out, it will then go to the printer. It usually takes from eight to ten weeks from this time until the first print run is received by the publisher. You now have a published book! You will receive a box in the mail one day containing the number of author copies promised in your contract.

Now, the hard work of promoting your title begins. (See the next chapter for more on promotion.) The first year, especially the first few months, of book sales is extremely critical, particularly when it comes to time-sensitive topics.

Be prepared to read reviews of your work in the professional literature, both positive and negative, with an open mind. While it can be disconcerting to see your book's flaws exposed by a reviewer, these comments can help you avoid pitfalls in your next work. Or, the reviewer might be completely off-base or having a bad day and taking it out on your work. Just remember the adage that any publicity is good publicity. Indulge yourself by clipping your positive reviews and sharing them with your family—and your editor!

Notes

1.   William Germano, *Getting It Published: A Guide for Scholars and Anyone Else Serious about Serious Books* (Chicago: University of Chicago Press, 2001): 2.

Chapter 10
Marketing and Promotion:
Yourself and Your Work

Librarians are often shy about marketing themselves and their work, but, as an author, you will need to overcome your inherent reluctance to self-promote. This is especially important if you have written a book, which will depend heavily on promotion and on good word-of-mouth for its sales. If you need an added incentive, remind yourself that the income you receive from book royalties is dependent on selling as many copies as possible of your latest title! You will always, however, wish to work on building your name recognition—even if you have not yet completed a monograph. The more well known you are, the more likely it is that you will be asked to participate in additional writing-related opportunities and the greater the impact your writing will have on your career as a whole.

Stephen King's latest title may receive a huge publicity push, including an author tour, full-page ads in the *New York Times*, online banner ads, and guest appearances on talk shows. Yours, unfortunately, will not. General publishing houses heavily promote only a few of their titles; library presses have an even smaller promotion budget—although you will have the advantage of very targeted publicity when and where they do promote their authors' work. While your publisher will provide your book with basic publicity, such as sending out review copies and press releases and listing it in its publications catalog, any more aggressive publicity efforts will often need to come from you.

You will need to promote your book-length work more than you will your articles. Articles have a built-in audience in the form of journal subscribers, and you do not depend on journal sales for royalties or incentive for a publisher to take on your next project. Therefore, the following sections will focus most heavily on steps you can take to promote your book(s), but will also discuss general ways of promoting yourself as a writer and getting your name out there.

Working with Your Publisher

Provide as much assistance as possible to your editor and your marketing (sometimes called "publicity") department as they begin the work of promoting your book. Give them all of the information and cooperation they request in order to market your title effectively—and then some! While you and your publisher both wish to sell books and to make money, yours is not their only title; they cannot afford to give the kind of concentration to promoting your work as you can. If you have ideas on promotion or contacts you can exploit, inform your editor and see if there is a way you can work together.

Luckily, most library publishers are smaller presses that will have more time to devote to working with authors and promoting titles than would their larger counterparts—as well as dramatically different notions of the meaning of sales success. (Library titles generally sell in such relatively small numbers that they are not appealing to general publishers.)

Your major responsibility to your publisher here lies in providing the material it needs for its marketing efforts. At some point during the publishing process, for example, you will be asked to fill out a marketing questionnaire for your title. This questionnaire includes a number of sections that all aim at eliciting information the publisher can use to promote your book. These sections typically ask for:

- Suggestions of potential review and advertising outlets for your work. Although the publisher will have standard review outlets to which it will send copies of your work, the assumption here is that your work and research in the field will give you a certain familiarity with journals and online sources of which the publisher may not be aware. Provide a list of all of the places that would ideally (and realistically) review your work. Reviews, especially in the library field, are one of the best ways of generating book sales. (Note that you will not receive royalties on review copies of your work, as these are not sales.)

- A short summary of your title. This provides an abstract the publisher can use in its cover and/or catalog copy, flyers, Web site, and other promotional material. Although this summary may be completely rewritten by the marketing department, you are giving them a guide to follow in creating an accurate description of your book. Make it short yet punchy, and ensure that it accurately reflects the contents and intention of your work.

- An author biography and photograph. These are again for use in marketing materials and in the book itself. Books, especially those in a specialized marketplace such as the library literature, often sell well based largely on the reputation and reliability of their author. This is not the place to be shy—list your qualifications, your degrees, and any experience or credentials that bear on the topic of your title. If you are asked to provide a photograph, the publisher will generally want a high-quality head shot and may or may not accept a scanned-in photo in place of the original.

- Suggestions for people to endorse your title. Here, provide the names of and contact information for well-known individuals in the field who may be willing to either endorse your work or to write a foreword for the book. This is where your previous networking activities will be important, as others will be more likely to lend their efforts if they have had previous discussions or contact with you. Pick people with both name recognition and expertise in your subject area. The publisher will be responsible for mailing galleys to these individuals, but you may be responsible for contacting them initially and ensuring that they follow through on any promise to provide endorsements. These endorsements are short, favorable quotes that can be used on the cover of your book as well as in advertising copy in catalogs, on flyers, and online (either on the publisher's Web site or on a page you create especially for this title). Quotes can help convince potential buyers of your work's merit.

- Special outlets for selling your work. Do you teach a course yourself, or is your book particularly suited for adoption as a textbook in library school classes? Do you intend to bring and sell copies when you make presentations to groups of information professionals?

- Basic author information. Give your name as you wish it to appear on the title and in cataloging data, your position and institutional affiliation, current contact information, and so on.
- Special features of your book. While it may seem odd to give the publisher information on a title it has in hand, realize that the marketing department and the people creating cover art, advertising copy, and so on for your book may not have read the title and depend on your descriptions to create accurate promotional material. Here, talk about any material that will be of particular interest to readers—has an artist created cartoons to illustrate each chapter? Does it include interviews with well-known figures in the field? Does it have a glossary outlining commonly confused technical terms relating to your topic?
- Newsworthy angles. The publisher will likely create a press release announcing the publication of your title and send it to the appropriate library outlets. If there are any particularly newsworthy angles relating to the book or yourself that should be included in such a release, list these here. The publisher may also ask for suggestions of places to announce your title, either in this section or in a separate question.
- The markets for your book. Yes, this repeats what you have previously outlined in your book proposal to the same publisher, but give the answer again here for the marketing department's use. You may also be asked here why the title will be of interest to each market or what benefits it will bring to a given audience. Again, you providing material they can use in creating a marketing plan for your book.
- Additional ways to market the title. List any special ways you will promote the work (through speaking engagements, on your Web site, by writing articles on the subject and including information on your title, and so on). Also list any additional suggestions you have for ways the publisher can help publicize the book.

While completing the marketing questionnaire may seem time-consuming and duplicative of the material in your initial proposal to the publisher, giving thorough attention to these questions allows the press to market your title most effectively. Remember that you and the publisher are partners in this effort and that their success in promoting the work depends on your cooperation and suggestions.

Ways in which your publisher may market your title include:

- Displays in their booth at professional conferences.
- Copy in their printed and online catalogs.
- Mailed flyers. They may also provide you with flyers and order forms to hand out at any presentations or workshops you conduct.
- Advertisements. This is especially true for publishers who also produce journals, such as Information Today.
- Review copies. The publisher will mail complimentary review copies to the most pertinent outlets. A good review can be one of the best ways to boost sales of your title.
- Press releases. Announcements should be sent to the major professional journals and to those specializing in the subject of your title.
- Their Web site. Many publishers highlight new titles prominently on their site, and some also post author interviews, sample chapters, or other value-added information.

You can add to these efforts through suggesting review outlets, providing copy the marketing department can use in describing your work, handing out flyers at your presentations, and linking to the publisher's Web site from your own.

Marketing through Professional Activities

All of your formal and informal professional activities also serve as built-in marketing opportunities for you and your work. These include speaking engagements, teaching classes or workshops, your posts on e-mail discussion lists, conversations with colleagues, your Web site, and articles you publish in the professional literature. Judith Siess, president of Information Bridges International, explains her strategy: "I mention the book(s) whenever I give a workshop or talk to a group. I mention them on my Web site and in my newsletter. It works."

Do not be shy about using professional activities as promotional opportunities. This does not mean that you should take every opportunity to blatantly advertise your work, but that you should make others aware when something you have published can help solve a problem or answer a question. You should also make it clear that you are available as a writer and as a speaker so that others looking for either know that they can turn to you.

One great way to do this is to attach a line promoting your other work to your bio whenever you write an article for the professional literature. Journals generally allow a couple of sentences at the end of

≡

s in which can you can include a Web site link, e-
r information on your latest title.

io line for a monthly "Computer Media" review col-
urnal, for example, read: "Rachel Singer Gordon is
library careers site Lisjobs.com and the author of *The*
Accidental Systems Librarian (Information Today, 2003)." This simple
statement gives readers a Web site to visit (which contains prominent
links to my résumé and information on my books), as well as information on my most recently published work. Those who make good use of
the reviews may be inspired to look me up.

This can be especially effective if you are able to repurpose some
of the material from your book or from a longer research article into
shorter, targeted articles for other journals. Many library authors rely
on the background and research they have done in completing a lengthy
project to also produce any number of shorter and more focused pieces.
Readers who are intrigued by your articles on a subject may be encouraged to seek out the longer or original work, and producing a number
of articles on a subject helps establish your reputation as an expert in
that field. However, you will wish to mention your book-length work in
any article bio, even if you are writing on an unrelated subject.

Take any opportunity to stay connected with your readers. You
can, for example, include your e-mail address in your books and in
your article bios and encourage your colleagues to contact you this
way. Ask for feedback on your work, or post or send out more formal
surveys soliciting others' opinions.

You can also promote yourself and your work in any material you
freely provide to other librarians. Librarian-turned-author Marylaine
Block creates a free e-zine that includes a weekly article on topics of
interest to librarians and a number of links to useful Web sites. Each
issue of her e-zine contains the note that this free service exists to promote her business as a writer and a speaker, and gives a link to outlines
of her previous presentations. Readers can easily see her writing style
and ability in the e-zine itself and are provided with a simple way to get
further information and to contact her.

Promote your writing through all of your professional activities. If
you are invited to present at a conference, hand out flyers on your latest
work or include information on your handouts. Feel free to cite your
own articles on material you hand out during your presentation, if they
are pertinent to the topic you are speaking on. Even attending professional conferences and networking with other attendees and presenters
can help your name recognition—also, be sure to stop by your publisher's booth and talk to your editor.

When you participate on e-mail discussion lists, consider putting information on your title in your signature, or post to provide a link to one of your articles or to your Web site if it answers a list member's question. (See chapter 11 for more on creating a Web site and promoting your work online.) Refrain here from blatant self-promotion, but provide information on your work in the context of the ongoing conversation and as a service to others.

Any professional activity that increases your name recognition and professional visibility helps promote you and your work, and increases the odds that you will be invited to do further projects. As you build your career, your books and articles will be read largely on the basis of your reputation. You want your readers eagerly to await your next book or your next column.

Just remaining active in the profession and maintaining a network of colleagues in your field will help you promote yourself and your writing. Word of mouth is tremendously powerful—you want those in your network telling everyone in their networks that they should buy your book or read your articles.

Remember that if you intend to make professional publishing an integral part of your library career, you are unlikely to stop with one book or one article. Cross-promote your own work; draw upon and cite your previous writing. As Levinson, Frishman, and Larsen emphasize: "The only time you can safely stop promoting your books is when you're ready to stop writing them."[1] Just as all professional communication is mutually reinforcing, so too do your professional activities and your writing work together in building your career and promoting your work—and yourself!

Notes

1. Jay Conrad Levinson, Rick Frishman, and Michael Larsen, *Guerrilla Marketing for Writers: 100 Weapons for Selling Your Work* (Cincinnati: Writer's Digest Books, 2001): 10.

Chapter 11
The Electronic Environment

The Internet has transformed library publishing just as it has influenced nearly every other area of librarianship. In most cases, the changes created by our new reliance on online tools are beneficial to authors. The electronic environment brings such advantages as:

- Allowing you to communicate quickly and easily with editors, publishers, and coauthors via e-mail.
- Supplying a built-in forum for soliciting feedback, posting surveys, and locating interviewees.
- Creating a new arena for your own and publishers' publicity and marketing efforts.
- Giving a place for editors to locate and evaluate potential authors.
- Providing an easy method of locating author guidelines for various publications and presses.
- Expanding your range of potential publishing outlets to include electronic journals and newsletters.
- Letting you locate publications online and evaluate them by reading either sample articles or full issues on the Web.
- Creating new opportunities for networking with colleagues and keeping current with professional issues, helping provide the foundation you need for successful writing.

There are specific strategies that will help you interact more effectively online, and the following sections provide you with the background you need to take full advantage of the medium in furthering your own library publication efforts.

You have no doubt also heard the by-now-tired cliché that the Internet makes everyone a publisher. This is true in one sense; as librarians have found to their chagrin in other contexts, anyone with minimal skills can post any content they desire to the Web. Yet, as we have also found, just posting on the Internet does not guarantee that anyone will find or read your writing—and the practice of self-publishing online denies you the benefit of professional editing and of getting an experienced publisher's perspective on your work before it is exposed to a wider audience. Professional writing still largely requires professional outlets.

A later section in this chapter, however, will describe how the online environment does provide an ideal forum for more informal professional communication and describes the exceptions to the online self-publishing rule. As more researchers and writers choose to bypass formal publication channels and self-publish online, either exclusively or in conjunction with their contributions to existing library outlets, Internet publishing does become a viable alternative—depending on the content and purpose of your writing.

Communicating Professionally Online

The Internet offers authors and editors improved avenues of communication, often entirely obviating the necessity to wait for communications to wend their way between parties via postal mail. Many publications now accept e-mailed queries and manuscripts, and using scanned-in artwork and screen captures can save you from having to mail original or photo-quality prints. The use of e-mail can help to speed up the publication process, both by reducing the need to mail manuscripts, galleys, and proofs between authors and editors and by allowing any questions or issues to be cleared up quickly. Electronic corrections of drafts and the ability to transfer Microsoft Word files as e-mail attachments eliminate the need to retype manuscripts and reduce the chance of miscommunication.

Recognizing the impact of the medium on the publishing world, most editors are now comfortable communicating online. Many even prefer e-mail to other forms of communication. The importance of remaining professional in all online communication, however, cannot be overstated—the sheer quickness and ease of e-mail may cause you to confuse messaging their editor with chatting with a friend. While your editor may eventually become a friend, it is inappropriate to cross that professional line, especially in your initial communications with him/her.

In order to interact effectively with editors online, aspiring librarian authors at the very least need to be comfortable with e-mail basics, including attaching files to messages, "zipping" together a number of documents and/or images into one file for easier transfer (see http://www.winzip.com), and creating professional e-mail signature files that point back to their own online presence. They also need to ensure that their antivirus software is up to date—Microsoft Word macro viruses and e-mail-borne viruses are common, and your editor will likely not take infection kindly.

Online collaboration tools also have opened up new opportunities for librarians to work together on books, articles, and other professional projects—even if they live in different parts of the world. Because of the ease and quickness of e-mail communication, geographically distant coauthors can share drafts and ideas nearly as easily as if they were conversing in person. Freely available chat client (or instant messaging) software from Yahoo!, Microsoft, AOL, and other vendors offers the additional option of real-time communication when remote coauthors need to hash out an issue, without incurring the cost of a long-distance phone call. Learning to collaborate effectively now often includes developing the skills needed to use these various forms of online communication. (For more on working with a coauthor, see chapter 6.)

E-mail Discussion Lists

Beyond one-to-one e-mail and instant messaging, other electronic opportunities for communicating with colleagues can be useful to aspiring authors. ALA's New Members Round Table, for example, sponsors an e-mail discussion list (NMRTWriter) for newer librarian authors, on which you can ask questions, find calls for contributors, and read advice from editors and more experienced writers. NMRTWriter also hosts scheduled discussions on specific subjects, such as finding collaborators and mentors and suggested paper topics. (To subscribe to NMRTWriter, send an e-mail message to listproc@ala.org. In the body of your message, type: subscribe nmrtwriter [firstname lastname].)

Table 11.1. Sample Call for Reviewers, *Reference Reviews*

CALL FOR REVIEWERS:

Librarians and other information professionals interested in evaluating electronic and print reference products for publication are invited to apply to be reviewers for *Reference Reviews (RR)*. *RR* is an international journal published eight times per year by Emerald (formerly MCB University Press). It is also available electronically to subscribers of the Emerald full-text journal service. For more information, please see http://www.emeraldinsight.com/rr.htm.

Individuals from all types of libraries (public, academic, special, school, etc.) are encouraged to apply.

Reviewers should be familiar with the subject area(s) in which they choose to review materials. In addition, reviewers of electronic products should know how to evaluate and navigate electronic resources, particularly Web sites and electronic databases. In addition, they should be able to write clearly and concisely. Attention to detail and deadlines is essential.

Typical reviews for *RR* run 500-800 words and are due approximately 30 days after assignment. Regular reviewers would be expected to contribute at least several times per year, depending on their schedules and the editor's needs.

Anyone interested is encouraged to drop me an e-mail note (address below). Please submit the following details:

- Name and complete contact information (title, snail mail, and e-mail addresses)
- Area(s) of subject expertise
- Previous publishing/reviewing experience, if any
- Brief description of your experience with electronic resources, if interested in electronic products

Thanks in advance for your interest, and please contact me with any questions.

Sarah L. Nesbeitt
Regional Editor (North America)
Reference Reviews
Booth Library, Eastern Illinois University
Charleston, IL 61920, USA
E-mail: cfsln@eiu.edu
http://www.emeraldinsight.com/rr.htm

Take advantage of such online forums to ask your questions about the publishing process in a nonthreatening environment. Also be on the lookout for calls for contributors or reviewers on NMRTWriter as well as on general e-mail discussion lists; editors have found that this is a quick and cost-effective way to get information on their publishing processes and current needs in front of large numbers of potential authors. See table 11.1 for an example.

The call for reviewers in table 11.1 appeared on the PUBLIB e-mail discussion list on November 2, 2002. Note that all applicable information appears in the body of the message: the requirements for reviewers, contact information for the editor, a description of the journal, requested query elements, and a Web site to consult for further information. When responding to any call for contributors or reviewers posted on an e-mail list, be sure to read the message carefully to locate all of these elements and to visit any Web site or other resource provided for further details. In your response, address each of the editor's requirements as laid out in her message.

So many librarians now participate online that calls for contributors posted on e-mail discussion lists may not even be repeated in the print literature or elsewhere; editors at many publishing outlets now find the online environment a more effective method of reaching potential writers and can fill their editorial needs entirely that way. Many librarians got their start in writing for publication by answering such a call for contributors, and outlets that post such requests online are also generally quite open to receiving queries or responses via e-mail. When the timing is right, it can be possible to see a call for contributors, query via e-mail, and receive an editor's response within the same day! (Although do not count on this happening; always give an editor a reasonable amount of time to respond before double checking to see that she or he received your query.)

Stay informed by subscribing to the major lists in your area of specialty, which also gives you the opportunity to see these calls for papers or articles. If the volume of messages grows overwhelming, change to the digest mode or make a habit of regularly browsing the list's online archive instead. (To locate lists, try "Library-Oriented Lists" at http://liblists.wrlc.org.) Calls for contributors can also be found online at sites such as Library Link's "Publishing Opportunities" page at http://www.emeraldinsight.com/librarylink/news/publishing.htm, a site that posts and reprints such messages for publishers. Also check the sites of individual journals; stay alert to these opportunities when browsing the sites of journals in your areas of interest.

Professional online communication on e-mail discussion lists and in related venues such as Web-based forums conveys additional advantages. Lists provide a natural place for editors to identify potential authors who are active in the profession, able to write, and knowledgeable in their field. Some editors prefer to cut down on inappropriate or unqualified submissions by actively soliciting individual writers for their publication rather than posting a general call for contributors or will supplement these more general requests by also asking people to write on specific topics. Posts on discussion lists and forums can in this way lead to contracts; editors often contact participants to see if they may be interested in expanding on their online messages by writing for their journal or publishing house.

A number of survey respondents note the serendipitous nature of these electronic contacts:

- "I had been posting to the Free Pint Bar (the forum affiliated with the *Free Pint News*, an online newsletter). One of their editors, Rex Cooke, noticed my posts and my place of employment, and asked if I'd be interested in doing an article on the influence of the Internet on patent practice."
- "I wrote a piece for the listserv PUBLIB, which I got several comments on. I then got an e-mail from *American Libraries* asking if I could expand that into an editorial."
- "I received a phone call from the Business & Economics editor of *CHOICE* magazine, asking me if I would be interested in reviewing books for *CHOICE* in the areas of business or economics. The editor knew my name and my experience from my role as editor of the BUSLIB-L e-mail list for business librarians."
- "In floating some ideas on public service and reserves via an e-mail listserv, I had an editor, who is active on the list, suggest that I write an article on the subject."
- "In one case I participated in a colloquy at the *Chronicle of Higher Education* Web site and an editor contacted me inviting an essay for the *Chronicle Review* based on a parenthetical remark I'd made in my posting. That piece, when it came out, has just sparked an invitation from a book publisher to consider sending them a book proposal. In short, this stuff snowballs."

Such contact shows the extent to which professional communication is intertwined and how the Internet is providing another venue to connect editors and potential authors. While participating online, remember always to conduct yourself professionally and to represent yourself well—you never know who might be reading! Since messages to many lists and forums are archived online, your comments can show up in Web search results as well. If editors are at a later date seeking experts on a particular topic, your name and posts may very well turn up as they look online for potential contributors.

Participation on lists also allows you to pick the brains of your fellow librarians when questions or issues arise in your writing. Since you are writing on professional topics, who better to ask than professional librarians? Most of your colleagues will be generous with their ideas and expertise; just be sure to keep your requests professional and to the point. You will of course have the best luck here when joining and posting your questions to the lists that are most relevant to the subject of your article or book; members of other lists may become irritated if your posts seem to be off topic.

Beyond participating in discussions of your article or book subjects on e-mail lists, you can use such lists to conduct surveys or to solicit respondents to online questionnaires. Freely available CGI scripts make it relatively simple to post a survey as an online form on your personal Web page and receive the responses in your e-mail box, or you can ask people to respond to a plain-text version via e-mail. (For more on creating and using surveys, see chapter 6.) Such questionnaires can also be a great way to find quotes to use in your writing and to learn the opinions of your colleagues, in the same way that quotes from the publishing survey respondents are reproduced throughout this book.

Lastly, discussion list and other online participation helps hone your writing skills and keep you connected to the profession—providing background for your later work as a librarian author. Gustavus Adolphus College Professor Barbara Fister suggests: "And while you're getting your nerve up [to submit your work to publishers], participate in appropriate discussion lists. It will polish your ability to express yourself in a low-risk, free-for-all environment and put you in touch with people who find your ideas interesting."

Publishing in E-Journals and Newsletters

Electronic journals and newsletters, while still relative newcomers compared to their more-established print counterparts, are gaining increasing respect and impact within the library community. While administrators and tenure committees previously were unsure, for example, how to evaluate electronic publication as a professional activity, writing for online publications is now becoming both more common and more recognized. Electronic publications are also beginning to be indexed and cited alongside their print counterparts. Some respected peer-reviewed journals are now published only online, and such newer journals have started to accumulate a track record that administrations can appreciate.

There are, however, inconsistencies in the way in which electronic publication is viewed and evaluated at different institutions, so you will wish to ascertain the preferences of those on your promotion and tenure committees if this is an issue for you. One survey respondent notes that: "Sadly, not enough academics respect the 'Net as a publishing place, possibly because they don't understand it. It's part of our job as librarians to educate them about this. It's not where it's published, it's the quality of the publication."

Especially when you are beginning your writing career, however, you cannot afford to ignore any potential outlet for your work—and librarians outside academia have less concern for the relative prestige or refereed status of electronic journals. Be sure to investigate publishing in online markets as well as in traditional print journals. Editors at online magazines, journals, and newsletters are also often more open to communicating entirely via e-mail, which will save you the postage costs and time associated with "snail-mail" letters and long-distance telephone charges. E-mail communication also often allows these editors to respond more quickly, which can help your work find more timely publication.

E-publishing outlets range from informal e-mail newsletters published by an individual or association subgroup to peer-reviewed academic journals put out by universities or associations. As in the offline environment, the appropriate outlet for your work depends on your intended audience and tone. While the nature of the medium does foster a tendency toward informality, again, you cannot interpret online publication itself as offering an invitation to communicate less than professionally. Even e-mail newsletters and other nonacademic outlets, which may actually encourage a certain sense of informality in their articles (such as first-person perspective, brevity, and lack of a strict research methodology), will nevertheless appreciate your professionalism when it comes to composing query letters, following guidelines, and working to deadline. Refereed e-journals will adhere to the same standards as their print counterparts.

Online newsletters and nonacademic journals are often more personally rewarding to write for. Contributors to such efforts tend to write because they have something to say to their colleagues or are passionate about an issue, rather than because they need credit for peer-reviewed publication. These types of publishing outlets offer you the opportunity to share practical insights with your fellow librarians and to write for the enjoyment of it.

Another advantage of having your work appear in electronic format is that online journals, especially those that make their archives freely available, may find a larger audience than many print publications. Particularly given the spiraling costs of scholarly publications, most institutions and individuals can afford to subscribe to relatively few traditional print journals. Their audience is therefore circumscribed, and articles in such publications may not reach those to whom they would be of greatest interest. A number of electronic journals, by contrast, make their content partially or entirely available to all visitors.

Marylaine Block emphasizes the importance of the increased availability of online material to scholarship as a whole, noting:

> We should consider the question of readership as well. The fact is, any journal article in even an esteemed scholarly journal will be read by a minute fraction of scholars in the field, and virtually not at all by students, hobbyists, and those who simply want to explore the subject. The very same article, if it's placed on the public Web and earns a high ranking, may be read by thousands, or even hundreds of thousands, of people, which can improve the general public's understanding of a topic or an academic discipline. You may think of this as a service contribution in tenure evaluations.[1]

This means also that your articles are likely to turn up when colleagues do a general Internet search on the subject, which will improve the visibility of your writing and contribute to your name recognition and career development. As CUNY Librarian Ann Grafstein explains: "I also find that when deciding where to publish, one of the things I look for are journals that have a strong electronic presence, rather than simply those with high circulation. My reasoning is that electronic access makes it more likely that your article will be read, discussed, and cited." Another academic librarian concurs, saying that "now, when considering where to submit an article, I am going to prefer journals for which full text is available online, as that will increase penetration."

This increased visibility holds true also for print journals that make selected articles available online. Yours may be one of these articles, and, even if not, a strong online presence means that the citation will be readily available for those who wish to dig further for a copy of the article itself. Both online-only journals and print publications with an online counterpart may at least post tables of contents and/or abstracts, which increases the visibility and findability of your work. Brewster Kahle, inventor of the "Wayback Machine" (http://www.archive.org), has an interesting take on this, asking: "How many subscribers does LexisNexis have? How many people use Google? Which would you rather publish in?"[2]

The flip side of this, however, is that there is little guarantee that a given electronic publication will continue publishing or maintaining its online archive. When print journals cease publication, there is a written record to turn to; however, when an online journal goes out of business, its Web site can easily disappear and its archives cease to exist. Take all these considerations into account when deciding where to submit your work, and be sure at least to maintain personal printed copies of every piece of work you publish online. (Print out the edited and formatted work after it appears, rather than relying entirely on your unedited originals.)

Look into the quality of any electronic outlet for your work. Since the barrier to creating an online publication is lower, the quality of such outlets can be more uneven than that of print journals, which need to justify publication costs such as printing and postage. Texas A&M Reference Librarian Catherine Collins comments: "Because it's cheaper, faster, and easier to publish on the Web, publishing opportunities have exploded over the last several years. There's an online publication for just about every topic and every audience. If you're too inexperienced to submit to one of the print periodicals or you can't seem to get your foot in the door, try one of the many online publications. Of course, the flip side is that there isn't uniform quality control on the Web, so it's the responsibility of the submitter to carefully evaluate these publications." This is another reason to become familiar with a publication before submitting your work.

Electronic publishers and the online counterparts of print journals often take advantage of the medium in other ways. They use the Internet to communicate with contributors, facilitate online communities of researchers, share information about their goals, provide tools to help writers succeed, and locate new authors. These initiatives include:

- At the online newsletter *Free Pint*, potential authors can sign up for the Author Update, a regularly e-mailed notice listing books available for review and ideas on ways to contribute. (Register at http://www.freepint.com/author.htm.) *Free Pint* also maintains online forums for information professionals, including discussions of issues raised in the newsletter.

- Emerald, which publishes a number of library and information science journals, maintains a "Literati Club" for authors and potential authors at http://www.emeraldinsight.com/literaticlub/. Sections include a research register, editing services for non-native English speakers, reprints, conference information, and articles on topics such as peer review and writing publishable papers.

- Elsevier maintains an online paper tracking site at http://authors.elsevier.com. There, you can also find out more about their journals and the publishing process as well as create a personalized page containing tracking information for your own papers, access to journals of interest, and ContentsDirect alerts that deliver tables of contents for books and journals to your desktop.

As use of the Internet becomes ever-more intertwined with our other professional activities, such online tools are sure to become a common aspect of library publishing. Become comfortable with their use and utilize the tools on publishers' sites to help you optimize your writing and research experience and manage your time more effectively.

Self-Publication Online

In many cases, it behooves you to have your work published by an existing outlet, whether on- or offline. Established publishers offer a number of advantages over attempting to self-publish online, including:

- *A built-in audience.* Unless you are already well known in the field, your colleagues lack any incentive to visit and read a privately created collection of work. Writing for a journal they already read, however, gets your name out there and your ideas in front of an existing audience.

- *Editing and proofreading service.* It is difficult to edit your own work; you are just too close to it. Established publishing outlets provide a second (and third, and fourth . . .) pair of trained eyes to help your work appear its best.

- *Evaluation.* Editors may be more aware of what has already been published on your subject and have the experience that will allow them to evaluate the merits of your work before you put something

potentially flawed or duplicative out there for the world to see.
They serve as gatekeepers to professional literature.

- *Status.* Tenure and promotion committees will be less impressed
  with self-publication than with peer-reviewed publication, and
  publication in an existing journal gives you another line for your
  résumé. Publication in a reputable journal or by a reputable press
  lends their authority and status to your work; self-published material depends entirely upon your own reputation.
- *Promotion.* Publishers will provide promotion for a book (see
  chapter 10) that can be very difficult for an individual to duplicate—or afford.

Consider these factors before choosing to self-publish rather than to
submit your work to others.

This being said, there are specific instances in which online self-
publication can be beneficial to your career. These include activities
such as creating a library-related Web log ("blog") or online newslet-
ter/e-zine, which provide you with a forum for more informal writing
while also helping you create your own online brand. These types of
publication can dovetail nicely with a more formal publishing career,
allowing you to promote your books and/or writing services to the
online audience you build up over time. (For more on marketing and
promotion, see chapter 10.) Note also that creations such as blogs and
newsletters offer a forum for more personal, informal online communication, their tone being a function of the genre. If you do establish an
online newsletter, help give it some legitimacy by applying for an ISSN
at http://www.loc.gov/issn/.

If you already have an established online presence, you can also
consider self-publishing e-books on your Web site. Those who intend
to sell these, however, will need to conquer the technological issues of
payment, copy protection, and distribution format. Publishing in electronic format allows you to bypass traditional publishers and ensures
your work will appear in a timely manner. As pre-DESIGN Planning
Associates President and Senior Consultant Matthew Simon notes:
"Publishing economics have made it more and more difficult for many
first-time writers to 'break-through.' Self-publication, either in print or
by making a publication available online, enables a writer—particularly
of a small market or niche monograph—to flank the obstacles that the
commercial press is increasingly throwing up."

Online writers do need to consider the unique needs of online
readers when writing for the electronic environment. Make the distinc-

tion between work meant to be printed out and that intended to be read on-screen, and remember that viewers' tolerance for reading online is much lower. Pay careful attention to your use of white space and make your work as concise as possible if it is meant for an online-only audience.

Alternatives to self-publication online are beginning to emerge for those who wish to publish their work, maintain creative control, and make their research available to others while bypassing traditional publishing outlets. One promising project in the library science field is DLIST, a repository of electronic resources in the fields of LIS and IT. (Visit the site at http://dlist.sir.arizona.edu.) Viewers are invited to browse DLIST freely and to contribute their own work to the archive.

Your Web Site

If you have created a Web site for information professionals, this provides another opportunity for you to post and/or link to your writing. If you have not, you should consider doing so—this is an inexpensive and simple way to highlight your writing and expertise in your field. A Web site is an especially great way to market your books. You can easily link to online bookstores or publishers' Web sites to allow visitors to purchase your title instantly. Library presses may post excerpts or sample chapters on their site that you can link to or provide you with edited and formatted versions you can post on your own. You can also link to any (favorable!) reviews of your title in online journals and newsletters and post quotes about its merits and a picture of the cover.

Also post value-added information for readers of the book, such as links to Web sites mentioned in the title, updated information, or related articles. This will keep them coming back to your site, where they can encounter other material you have published or be encouraged to use your services as a speaker or writer. You can also provide easy ways for readers to contact you via e-mail or an online form, remaining accessible to and open to dialogue with site visitors. (Be sure to answer the e-mail that you receive!) Visit the Web sites of some library authors you admire for ideas on how to create a useful Web presence. You can cross-promote here by also mentioning your Web site in your book (in the "About the Author" statement, introduction, or wherever it best fits).

In many cases, you will not wish to post a good deal of original work on your Web site, partially because some traditional publishing outlets consider even posting an article on a personal site to be a form of publication. If you choose later to submit work which has already appeared online, these journals will not accept it as an original article but instead view it as a reprint. Be cautious about posting articles on topics you may wish to later explore in an established journal.

Also be cautious about posting original research on the public Web unless you are comfortable with the possibility of your ideas being shared with (or even co-opted by) others. While you should balance this fear with a commitment to sharing ideas and knowledge with your peers, you will want to maintain your ownership of original research and to receive proper attribution when others use your work. You may wish to investigate self-licensing schemes such as those from Creative Commons (http://creativecommons.org) or other innovative ways of licensing and distributing your work.

There are times when you will wish to use your Web site to publish original material. If you have written a book for library professionals, for example, you can post articles on related topics to help draw readers in to the subject and advertise the additional material available in the fuller work. If you are tremendously prolific, you can post those articles you wish to keep control and copyright of and which you are not intending to submit to any professional publication. If you have something you wish to say to the profession and you do not care about having it published in the print literature, post it on your site; you can also use a personal site to publish articles which are too controversial for the traditional library media. If you are using your Web site to promote your services as a speaker, you can post articles to support your claim of expertise or to advertise your viewpoint on particular issues, as well as handouts or PowerPoint slides from previous presentations. If you have created an online newsletter, it can serve as an outlet for your own work, with you as editor. If you have time-sensitive work you wish to publish, self-publication allows you to bypass the lengthy peer-review process.

Personal Web sites also provide a venue for pathfinders, bibliographies, and other materials that are published in the print literature less often than in the past and for work that would lose its freshness by the time it went through the publishing process and finally appeared in the print literature. One survey respondent notes that:

> I now have the option to "publish" either in print or electronically. I also can choose to bypass the whole peer-review process and probably reach an even wider audience by directly posting my writings on the Web. Certain genres (e.g., short topical bibliographies) have pretty much disappeared from the formal journal literature and live

Table 11.2. Online Scholarship Efforts and News

DLIST
  http://dlist.sir.arizona.edu

FOS News Weblog
  http://www.earlham.edu/~peters/fos/fosblog.html

The Free Online Scholarship Newsletter
  http://www.earlham.edu/~peters/fos/

Scholarly Electronic Publishing Bibliography
  http://info.lib.uh.edu/sepb/sepb.html

SPARC (The Scholarly Publishing and Academic Resources Coalition)
  http://www.arl.org/sparc/

---

only on the Web now. . . . On the other hand, Web publishing offers many more opportunities to ease into the whole writing and publishing routine. And it is easier to get rid of your mistakes—just update the site or pull the page off the Web! Finally, the Web has the potential . . . to significantly reduce the lag time between submission and appearance.

Use your best judgment when it comes to posting original work.

You do, however, want to use your Web presence to allow others to access and read your work. The best way to do this is to post links to your previously published articles or book excerpts when these are made available online by the publisher. Many journals now make some or all of their content available on the Web, which makes it simple to add links to your articles from your site or from your online résumé. If your article is not among those available at the journal's site, ask your editor for permission to post a copy on your own Web site; the journal may even provide you with an edited version in Microsoft Word or Adobe Acrobat format.

Research, Reading, and Peer Review

The Internet holds the potential to keep librarians informed and involved in their profession. Just as journals that make content freely available online can increase the visibility of your writing, these publications also allow you the opportunity to remain informed and involved, even if your institution subscribes to relatively few print publications. One survey respondent exclaims: "I think that the Internet is definitely transforming the publishing process. It has made it much easier for us as a profession to explore and exchange professional ideas through a vastly popular technology. It makes published articles much more accessible to many—you don't have to subscribe to tons of journals nowadays to have access to some very valid and interesting information from some of the most dedicated and exhilarated members of the library/information science profession. I think that this is awesome!"

Librarians can subscribe to current-awareness publications such as *The Informed Librarian,* a monthly e-mail newsletter that links to the tables of contents of hundreds of online library and information-related journals, magazines, 'zines, and newsletters, gives editor's picks of recommended articles, and includes reviews of new titles in the field (http://www.infosourcespub.com/book4.cfm). Other publishers such as Haworth and Emerald provide electronic table of contents awareness services for their own journals and monographs.

The electronic environment also holds the potential to transform the peer-review process. One ongoing concern about the peer-review process has been the delay in publication it causes, which can cause research results to seem out-of-date as soon as they are published or ruin the timeliness of an article topic. The traditional length of the process is partially attributable to the time spent mailing manuscripts between far-flung volunteer reviewers, editors, and authors. Web- and e-mail-based review systems hold the potential to cut down considerably on the time, cost, and administration of peer-review programs at many journals.

Web-based systems can allow authors to track the progress of their manuscripts online. A common complaint among writers for peer-reviewed publications involves the uncertainty about where an article might be in the publication pipeline. Tracking systems let authors follow the progress of their work through the system without having to continually check with their editor.

Electronic Ethics

As countless schoolteachers and professors have found to their chagrin, the Internet has the unfortunate capacity to facilitate the borrowing of others' ideas, often resulting in outright plagiarism. Librarians as authors should be both more ethical and more savvy.

One survey respondent stresses: "Do detailed research before submitting your piece(s); give an accurate bibliography with credit to the authors who have written on your topic previously. Ethics is a serious thing in publishing."

The ease with which material can be accessed and copied from the Internet can encourage a certain sloppiness in research. It is easy to copy and paste information into your document while you are working, and it is also easy to forget to take down a full citation or to make proper attribution. While using electronic sources in your research and writing, make a special effort to keep accurate records and provide citations for the work you draw upon. Give the same credit as you would appreciate when other librarians draw on your own work.

Notes

1.   Marylaine Block, "Web Contributions and Tenure Decisions," *Ex Libris* 159 (November 14 2002), http://marylaine.com/exlibris/xlib159.html (20 November 2002).
2.   Brewster Kahle, "Way Back When," *New Scientist.com*, http://www.newscientist.com/opinion/opinterview.jsp?id=ns23701 (27 November 2002).

Chapter 12
The Business of Publishing

Library publishers, just like their larger counterparts, are in business to sell books, journals, and/or ad space—and, ideally, to make money. Throughout the publishing process, they will be looking out for their own interests; yours will be represented to a lesser extent. This requires that you take the time to educate yourself about the business of publishing, from reading and interpreting contracts to understanding the jargon of the industry. Understanding publishing as a business will also help you talk editors' language and understand your own obligations in convincing a publisher of the market/audience for your book or article.

You will also need to understand the essentials of treating your own writing as a business, from setting aside money from your freelance endeavors for taxes to deducting allowable expenses. Understanding the business of writing is especially important if you publish a book, as you will be responsible for paying taxes on royalties (just as you would on any other income) and will need to read and sign a contract with your publishing house before they will agree to publish your work.

If you have previous experience publishing in the library environment, you by now realize that your endeavors are not likely to make you wealthy. Peer-reviewed publications, in particular, tend to assume that the professional benefits that accrue from being published are reward in themselves, while more general journals may only pay a token stipend. Library-related monographs, because of their limited market, sell in much smaller quantities than general trade publications, with correspondingly smaller royalty checks. Still, any additional earnings are welcome—especially on a librarian's salary!—and must be declared to the IRS like any other income.

Note while reading this chapter that I am neither a lawyer nor an accountant, that tax and copyright law is subject to change, and that laws and tax information outside the United States may differ considerably from what is presented here. Always consult a lawyer with experience in publishing law or an accountant for professional and up-to-date information when necessary; the information in this chapter serves only as a general guide. Neither Scarecrow Press nor Rachel Singer Gordon will be liable for damages incurred from following the advice presented in this chapter.

The Book Contract

Once a publisher has accepted your book proposal, you will be mailed a copy of its standard author contract to sign. Always remember that any contract is negotiable—you are free to disagree with the publisher on certain points, remembering that a final, mutually agreeable contract is what you both want. Some publishing houses' standard contracts include terms that are less than fair to their writers, their hope of course being that (especially inexperienced) authors will sign anything just for the possibility of seeing their work in print.

Be sure that you have read and understood the contract before signing; do not sign away the world just for the chance to see your book published. Most library publishers are smaller and will be more flexible than larger houses. Be sure also that any changes you agree on to the standard contract are initialed and that the amended contract is signed by both you and the publisher.

The basic purpose of any contract is to spell out the rights and responsibilities of the parties involved. The basic intention of a publishing contract is to grant a publisher the exclusive right to publish your book, guarantee you that the publisher will publish your (acceptable) manuscript, and delineate both parties' rights and responsibilities. A standard publishing contract covers several main areas, including but not limited to:

- Royalties. Author royalties are based on a percentage of the net price of the book, generally not on the cover price. "Net" here means the monies received by the publisher from the sale of the book (after discounts). Your contract will state this percentage, how often you will receive statements and payment, whether the percentage varies when a certain number of books have been sold or if foreign rights are sold, and so on. Royalties from library publishers generally range from 10 to 15 percent and will be paid out once or twice yearly. Some publishers pay royalties on a sliding scale, for example, you may receive 10 percent on the first 1,000 copies sold, then 12.5 percent on each copy sold thereafter. Try to avoid writing original manuscripts for a flat fee (a "work for hire" agreement); instead, look for a royalty agreement—if your book takes off, you will never see another penny unless you are receiving a percentage of each sale. This clause should also explain how often royalties will be paid and sales will be reported, and, either here or in a separate clause, you (or your representative) should be given the right to audit the publisher's records on your book's sales performance.

- Advance. An advance is just what it sounds like: an advance payment on expected royalties on your book. If you receive an advance, you will not receive royalties on your title until you earn back what you have already been paid. Most publishers in the information science field will not pay an advance. If one does offer an advance, or if you negotiate one, it will generally be fairly small, and is often paid half upon signing of the contract and half upon receipt of an acceptable manuscript. Library-related titles have a smaller market than general trade books, with correspondingly smaller sales, so your publisher will not want to pay out more than it reasonably expects you to earn back. Also note that if you fail to finish or turn in your manuscript, you will need to repay the advance money to the publishing house.

- Copyright. Publishers may include a clause in the contract stating that they will register copyright to your work in their own name. You, on the other hand, may want to maintain copyright in your own name. Many publishers will negotiate on this point. Regardless of who holds copyright, however, the publisher will maintain the explicitly spelled-out rights that you assign to it by signing the contract. Copyright should be registered within three months of publication.

- Rights. The publisher will usually ask for "all rights" to the work, in "all formats." These generally include electronic rights, the right to publish in other languages and countries, subsidiary rights, and the right to serialize the work and to publish it in another format (such as paperback, for example). Some of these rights are less important in library publishing; you are unlikely, for example, to see your work produced as an audio book. This clause will also delineate how any profits from foreign sales, reprinted excerpts, etc., will be split between you and the publisher.

- Due date. When will the manuscript be completed and due at the publisher? You should have discussed this with your acquisitions editor prior to receiving the contract and have arrived at a mutually agreeable date. Be sure to leave yourself sufficient time to complete the manuscript; do not try to be overly ambitious here. Many publishers are flexible, and if you find that the writing process is taking longer than expected, you can negotiate a new date—even after the contract has been signed. If you do find you need to change your date, however, talk to your editor as soon as possible. (This means that you need to bring up the issue more than a week or two before the manuscript is expected at the publisher!) If you do not complete the manuscript by the deadline or fail to complete it at all, you will have to return any advance against royalties the publisher has paid. This clause will also state that the manuscript must be "satisfactory"—this is up to the discretion of the publisher. A publisher must accept or reject your work within a certain date of delivery, which should be spelled out here, and should offer you a set period of time to rewrite and resubmit your manuscript before rejecting it outright.

- Preparation of the work. Are you expected to provide a full printout of the book, files in MS Word (or similar) format, or both? Are you expected to send multiple copies? What is the expected length of the manuscript?

- Competitive works. The publisher will ask you to agree not to write a directly competing work, usually for as long as this title is in print. You want to make sure that "directly competing" is defined explicitly, so as not to limit your future writing career. You may also wish to make sure that "in print" is defined fairly— sometimes publishers will specify that a title is in print so long as a single copy remains unsold in their warehouse, even if they are making no further efforts to reprint and/or sell the title. When the title goes out of print, all rights should revert back to you, and this should be explicitly stated in the contract as well.

- Revised editions. This clause should state that you will have the first opportunity to write a revised edition, but may state that the publisher can find a new author if you are unwilling or unable to revise the work at a later date.

- Author copies. How many copies of the finished work will you receive for free, and what discount do you receive if you wish to purchase additional author copies? Publishers generally provide between five and twenty author copies, and around a 40 percent author discount.

- Indemnification and warranties. This is where you promise that this is your original work, that you have not previously published it or assigned any rights elsewhere, and that you will not break the law by defaming others, plagiarizing, or so on. The publisher will want to be sheltered from any lawsuits that might stem from you doing any of these things, and will likely state that you, not they, are liable in this instance.

- Permissions. Who will be responsible for securing permissions and providing any necessary payments to copyright holders for added material (photographs, charts, excerpts . . .) you wish to include in your book? Generally the publisher will want you to pay for any permissions, although they will often supply forms for you to use in securing agreement. If you are responsible for the cost of securing permissions, you may need to limit your use of copyrighted material. Some publishers will accept e-mailed permission for the inclusion of material such as interviews you conduct. Permissions will most likely be due at the publisher along with your final manuscript.

- Indexing. Will you be responsible for indexing your own work, or will the publisher hire an indexer? Indexing your own writing can be more difficult than you may imagine. If the publisher does hire an indexer, will they take the fees out of your royalties? If so, be sure that a reasonable limit (usually around $500) is set in this clause.

- Publication of the work. This clause includes the time the publisher has in which to publish the work (generally a year or so after receipt of the manuscript), and explains what happens if they decide not to publish it after all (rights should revert back to you so that you can take your manuscript elsewhere). This clause generally will say that the book will be published in the manner and style the publisher chooses, which gives them leeway in such matters as design, cover, price, and so on.

- Bankruptcy and insolvency. This clause protects you in the event the publisher should go out of business or declare bankruptcy. In this event, all rights to your work should revert back to you.

Most general books on writing will include a section on contracts, and many show sample contracts and describe each clause thoroughly. You may also wish to consult online resources such as Publaw.com.

Be on the lookout for arrangements such as "work-for-hire" agreements, in which the publisher agrees to pay you a flat sum in exchange for your work on a manuscript. In this case, you are never entitled to any royalties, even if the book should later become a library literature bestseller. You will normally not wish to sign a contract of this type, unless you are taking on a revision project or other project that is similarly limited in scope. Note also that in work-for-hire cases the publisher owns the copyright of and all rights to the work as if they had created it, and you will need to agree to this provision in writing. Be aware and be sure that you are receiving fair compensation for your work and time.

Some journals will also require their authors to sign a contract prior to their work's publication. This will be similar in appearance to the book contract, although shorter and generally less involved. A number of academic journals, in particular, will require authors to sign over copyright to their work and will include an indemnification and warranties clause. Other journals may ask only for "first North American" (or other regional) serial rights. This gives the journal the right to be the first publisher to publish the work in the region, and all other rights to the work (including the ability to resell it, post it in electronic format, and so on) are reserved to you. If you create a piece that is to appear in a collected work, you will also be asked to sign a contract giving the publisher the right to print your work in that collection.

Taxes and Accounting

Keeping accurate track of your expenses and payments for tax and accounting purposes will become more important as you tackle larger and potentially more lucrative projects such as monographs, or if you begin writing regularly for a journal that compensates you for your work. Remember that expenses incurred directly from the process of writing are deductible, and keep any receipts.

Expense items can include:

- Postage. If you mail out a survey, or if you are required to mail printouts of your manuscripts to your publisher, keep track of these transactions.
- Photocopying fees. If you spend a few dollars reproducing your book manuscript at Kinko's, keep the receipt.
- Phone charges. If you incur long-distance charges when conducting interviews with remote contacts, keep the itemized bills and mark the appropriate portions.
- Research expenses. This will be applicable if you are conducting a large-scale research project for which you must travel or incur other expenses. Itemize and document these.
- Permissions. If you pay for permission to use a chart, lyric, or other content, keep documentation on these fees.

While such deductions may seem small individually, you may be surprised at the end of the year by how much you have spent to support your writing. Any deduction is useful when it comes to dealing with the IRS. If you intend to make a regular habit of writing, you can investigate other options such as the home-office deduction, but be aware that rules regarding these types of deductions can be complex.

You will also need to keep records of all writing-related income you receive during a given tax year. Be sure to keep records of any income as you receive it, which will make it easier to collect your information and do taxes at the end of the year. (If you receive regular writing-related income, consider setting up an Excel spreadsheet or other electronic method of organizing this information.) Your income from writing includes:

- Honoraria. If you receive any payment for articles you have written, you will need to declare it as income.
- Royalties. This also includes any advance you may receive from a library publisher toward future royalties. Publishers will send regular statements of sales and royalties, which you can use to keep track of such income for tax purposes. You will also receive a 1099 form during tax season from each publisher that has paid you over $600 during the course of the previous year.
- Monetary awards.
- Grants. Most grant monies, if awarded to you personally rather than to your institution, will be treated as earned income by the IRS.

IRS forms you should familiarize yourself with include Schedule C ("Profit or Loss from Business") to form 1040, Schedule SE ("Self-Employment"), and the quarterly 1040-ES ("Estimated Tax for Individuals").

If you anticipate owing a significant amount to the IRS at the end of the year on royalties and/or other writing-related and freelance income, you will want to pay estimated taxes on a quarterly basis in order to avoid penalties. You can also consider revising the W4 that you have on file with your regular employer in order to have extra taxes deducted from each paycheck and help avoid this kind of unpleasant surprise at the end of the year. You will owe both federal and state income tax (where applicable) on this income, at the percentage appropriate to your tax bracket. Your writing-related income can also push you up a tax bracket, so be aware of this possibility.

Realize also that you will still owe Social Security and medicare taxes (FICA) on this income, just as if you were working for an employer. You will be subject to self-employment tax on these earnings. This means that you will need to pay both your own and your "employer's" share of these taxes—since you are in this case self-employed, you are in effect paying both shares. The self-employment tax currently runs around 15 percent.

Copyright and Permissions

When planning out your book project, try to decide at the outset if you intend to reproduce any portions of others' work in your own. Beyond brief quotes, which are protected by the concept of "fair use," you will need to get permission from the copyright holder or holder of rights to the work to reprint or reproduce excerpts, photographs, charts and so on. There are no hard-and-fast guidelines for fair use, but, if you are quoting extensively from another's work (around 300 words, or most of a printed page), you will want to request permission to reprint the excerpt. If you are quoting any portion of song lyrics or a poem, you will wish to request permission. Leave as much time as possible to request and receive this permission; send your requests out early.

Get permission in writing. Your publisher may provide you with a boilerplate letter you can use to request permission to use others' work; simply fill in the pertinent information and you are ready to go. Otherwise, a number of writing guides and legal guides provide samples that you can modify for your own use. See table 12.1 for an example

Table 12.1. Sample Permission Letter

Dear [copyright holder, permissions manager]:

I am writing to request permission to reprint the following material from your publication [author, title, date, page number]. This material is to appear in the following work, tentatively titled [title] and to be published by [publisher] in [date].

Unless you indicate otherwise, credit will be given in the work to [author, title, publisher]. I am requesting nonexclusive world rights in all languages and in all editions.

Please sign below and return this form to me. I am enclosing an additional copy for your records.

If these rights belong to someone else, please advise me to whom I should forward this request.

Thank you for your consideration,

[name]

The request for permission to reprint the material described above, under the conditions outlined, is approved.

Name: _____   Date: _____

Signature: _____

of a typical permission letter. This letter generally lists the title and publisher of your work and asks for nonexclusive world rights in all languages to reproduce the excerpt, photograph, or other item in that work. You will want to send it to the permissions department of the publisher of the work; they should be able to advise you if rights have reverted back to the author or if some other party holds the rights to the material.

Realize that many rights holders will charge a fee for the use of their work in your own. Payment of these fees will usually be your responsibility, so be selective in what you choose to use. You can also check the Copyright Clearance Center at http://www.copyright.com to see if the work you need permissions for is registered, and then request permission through them.

If you choose to self-publish your own work on your personal Web site or elsewhere, you own copyright to that work as soon as it is written down. Others must have your permission to reproduce that work. To reinforce this concept, place the copyright symbol, first date of publication, and your name at the bottom of the Web page where your work appears, such as: © 2003 Rachel Singer Gordon. You may wish to make a habit of regularly searching for key phrases from your work online to see if another site has improperly reproduced your writing.

You can also register your work with the copyright office yourself, which provides you with evidence and a date that your work was registered with the office in the case of copyright infringement. Registration is a prerequisite to filing a copyright infringement suit. If you place a book with a publisher, the publisher should register the work for you. For more on U.S. copyright and permission provisions or to obtain copyright registration forms, visit the Copyright Office online at http://www.loc.gov/copyright/.

While thinking about contracts, taxes, and copyright is the least exciting part of writing, it is necessary to a smooth library publishing career. Temper the time you spend on these matters with the excitement you find in creating your work, and find your balance as a successful librarian author.

Appendix A
Writing for Publication Survey

Thanks for taking the time to complete this short survey about your experiences with publishing in the library literature. By filling out this survey, you are giving your permission to be quoted in a forthcoming book from Scarecrow. (If you would like to remain anonymous, please note that in your answers. Identifying details about your institution will then be deleted from any quoted answers as well.) If questions do not apply, please leave them blank.

Your name:

Your e-mail address:

Your employer:

Your job title:

Would you like your answers to remain anonymous? (Y/N)

What gave you the idea for your first published piece in library literature? How did you decide where to submit your idea, and where and when did it appear?

Is publication important in achieving tenure or promotion in your institution? (Y/N)

If yes, please explain how publication contributes: Is it required for tenure? Is it a possible factor along with other professional activities? Is peer-reviewed publication necessary?

Has an editor ever contacted you to inquire if you would be interested in writing for his/her journal/press? (Y/N)

If yes, please explain how and why this came about.

How do you feel professional publication has contributed to your career advancement?

What one piece of advice would you give another librarian interested in having his/her work published in the library literature?

Have you ever written a book on a topic related to librarianship? (Y/N)

If yes, please tell a little bit about your experiences with writing a monograph: Did you find it more difficult than writing articles? Did anything surprise you about the process? How did you go about marketing your title?

Do you feel that the Internet is transforming the publishing process? Why/why not?

Is there anything else you would like to share about your experiences writing for publication?

Appendix B
Publisher Interviews

Interviews were conducted during the summer and fall of 2002 with several publishers at a representative variety of library outlets.

American Libraries

Could you talk a little bit about the type of articles that appear in American Libraries, *and their length, format, and style?*

News and feature articles about issues and trends in libraries are the mainstay of *American Libraries*. Feature articles are generally no longer than 1,500 words. *AL* style is journalistic, not scholarly. The best source for this information is at http://www.ala.org/Content/NavigationMenu/Products_and_Publications/Periodicals/American_Libraries/Submitting_articles/Default604.htm.

How does the magazine differ from other major publications in the field?

American Libraries has the largest circulation, over 65,000, and it presents extensive news and coverage of the activities of ALA. The news section is the largest in the profession and consists of independent reporting of hard news.

Do you actively solicit article contributors to American Libraries, *or does most freelance content originate from author queries?*

Probably a quarter of the articles published in *AL* have been acquired based on a query. Perhaps one an issue is solicited. The rest arrive over the transom.

How much of the magazine is freelance written?

More than half, including departments, features, and special reports.

What advice would you give to newer writers who were interested in contributing to the magazine?

Start with a carefully crafted letter to the editor for "Reader Forum."

Do you have certain departments that are particularly open to newer authors, or are there particular types of articles you are looking for?

In addition to letters to the editor, the "On My Mind" page often features newer writers who have a strong opinion to express. The best place to break into writing, however, may not be *American Libraries*. A newsletter or a smaller, more targeted journal may be a more appropriate choice.

Do you prefer that potential contributors query first, or that they send completed manuscripts for consideration?

Either way is fine. We are happy to reply to queries with suggestions and direction, but we receive many completed manuscripts that end up in the pages of *AL*. A look at recent issues and the editorial calendar can help writers aim articles more appropriately. See http://www.ala.org/al_onlineTemplate.cfm?Section=Submitting_article s&Template=/ContentManagement/ContentDisplay.cfm&ContentID=2 449.

How does the publishing process proceed after a manuscript or query is submitted?

Several editors read the manuscript and recommend whether or not to acquire it, based on its quality and how it fits into the editorial calendar. The process can take a month or more, depending on how quickly we can decide that it fits into a forthcoming issue.

Approximately what percent of submissions to American Libraries *are accepted?*

About 10 percent.

What is your most common reason for rejecting an article?

It is not written for *American Libraries*. The author seems not to have matched the piece with the magazine and seems to have no sense of the scope or tone of *American Libraries*.

What changes has American Libraries *made to adapt to the electronic environment?*

A portion of the magazine is available online, as well as weekly news stories, which later make their way into print. Much more communication is done by e-mail. All submissions must sooner or later be turned into an electronic version.

How do these changes impact writers?

Access and communication are faster and more convenient. It has also given them a lot to write about!

How large is American Libraries' *readership?*

Sixty-five thousand subscriptions, one hundred thousand readers.

Is there anything else you'd like to share about the publishing process at American Libraries?

My best advice to writers is to get to know the magazine they want to write for. Remember that the editors are putting together a monthly product from hundreds of sources. Try to match what you are proposing with the place you see it occupying in the magazine. The best writers are the most astute readers.

Leonard Kniffel is editor and publisher, *American Libraries.*

Library Journal (Book Review Section)

Please describe the content and format of Library Journal *book reviews. What do you look for in an ideal review?*

    LJ book reviews are intended to help librarians decide which books to purchase for their collections. They typically consist of three parts: 1) a summary of the book's content and the author's credentials, 2) an evaluation of that content, 3) and a recommended audience. In terms of recommendations, the reviewer should point out the importance of the topic itself and the book's level of treatment (e.g., general, scholarly). If the topic is strictly for a popular audience, for instance, the book would be recommended for public libraries. If the book is on a more challenging subject but deemed highly accessible, it may then be recommended for both public and academic libraries. If the treatment demands a level of knowledge beyond the average lay reader or investigates issues of concern primarily to students and/or researchers, the book would be directed to academic libraries. Whenever possible, we ask reviewers to compare the book at hand with one or two alternatives in the recommendation. This comparison may consider quality, e.g., the book reviewed does a better job than other titles, and/or in terms of approach, e.g., the book takes a more personal or academic or cursory approach to the topic. If it's the only book on an important subject or a ground-breaking book on a much-documented subject, that should be mentioned.

    Given their practical function and the shortage of space in the magazine, reviews should be concise and brief (150-200 words for fiction and nonfiction, 100-150 in most columns, 225-250 for a composite of two books, 250 for reference).

    All in all, there isn't a lot of room or need for literary pyrotechnics, but like most readers, we editors enjoy a clever turn of phrase, humor in the right context, and especially a distinct "voice"—just the sense that the reviewer is writing with authority and confidence. The best reviews fulfill the three *LJ* requirements as well as surprise and engage. The most common mistake reviewers make is to get caught up in describing the book and forget to offer an opinion.

What do new reviewers find most challenging about the process?

Novices struggle with the brevity of our reviews. Conciseness is an art; it takes time and practice to learn how to summarize and evaluate a book in 150 to 200 words.

How do you identify potential new reviewers for the publication? Are you open to using reviewers with little previous publication or reviewing experience?

We print ads in the magazine and post some online asking interested persons to submit a résumé and two writing clips, and then we sift through the responses. Strong candidates will have an MLS (so that they understand the concepts of budget and audience), academic degrees in their reviewing field of choice, previous writing/reviewing experience, knowledge of the publishing world, and willingness to cooperate with an editor.

Those with slim portfolios are welcome to submit, as long as they can demonstrate good writing skills and patience, as learning our format takes time. I have worked with recent MLS and non-MLS graduates alike, and within six months to a year, they evolved into highly serviceable reviewers.

We always ask potential reviewers to submit two sample reviews. Aside from showing us that the candidate can write and evaluate, the sample review shows the candidate herself whether she is indeed interested in reviewing. Probably half the people who query us about reviewing never complete the application process because once they try writing a review, especially a short one, they realize that it is harder work than they thought or just not to their liking.

Do you specifically look for subject experts to review books in a particular field?

Certainly, but they are hard to find and keep because they usually have a lot on their plate. All our reviewers, however, have basic knowledge and training in their fields, whether through academic study, personal reading, or collection development experience. People can and do evolve into experts by constant reading and reviewing in a particular area, but they always start with a basic knowledge of the area.

What advice would you have for librarians interested in reviewing for LJ—*or for other library publications?*

I would recommend that prospective reviewers take a good, hard look at their schedules. Book reviewing eats up time and mental energy, so if you already have three other priorities, reviewing for *LJ* may be too much—especially since we don't pay. That said, it helps if you possess a passion for books, reading, and communication. Those who don't often fall off the wagon shortly after starting. In addition, candidates should take a good, hard look at the various publications and decide which might suit their writing style and interest. Some people will find the longer *Choice* reviews or *Booklist's* more popular orientation and policy of endorsement more to their liking or experience. *LJ* strives for balanced, thoughtful reviews that nevertheless offer criticism where criticism is due, and we have no problem with running reviews that say "not recommended." So reviewers who are hesitant to be critical or who are eager to show off their knowledge at the expense of the book don't work for us.

What professional advantages accrue to librarians who add book reviewing to their résumé?

Aside from the simple pleasure of expressing one's ideas—and of seeing the upshot in print—reviewing can and does help reviewers professionally. On a résumé, the reviewer's credential serves to demonstrate expertise in a given field, ability to articulate one's ideas, and a willingness to serve the larger library community. Reviewers frequently ask *LJ*'s editors for recommendations. Finally, the signoff guarantees name recognition within a community, leading to offers within and without the library world, e.g., job opportunities, invitations to speak, and acknowledgment at conferences, as well as offers to review for the local papers, for instance.

Do your reviewers ever go on to do other, larger projects for Library Journal?

Yes, very frequently. Most often, they take on collection development articles or features dealing with a particular facet of library science. Four of my regular reviewers have graduated to feature writing. One has gone on to write a column. It's a natural progression.

What are the particular challenges in reviewing fiction versus review-ing nonfiction materials?

Fiction is problematic because it provokes such visceral reactions. Novels often break rules, bend truths, and twist expectations, so they must be evaluated on their own terms. Sometimes as a reader, you are somewhere among love, indifference, and disgust, and it's hard to find the words to crystallize that. That's where we editors come in. We do our best to help reviewers articulate that misty place in their minds. Often that results in several drafts.

With nonfiction, on the other hand, it's often a question of whether the author clearly communicated her thesis and sufficiently backed it up with research and interviews, etc. We want our reviewers to have both the knowledge to judge an author's arguments and the ability to judge fairly, praising what deserves praise and critiquing weaknesses without bending over backwards in either direction and with an aware-ness of one's own personal biases. The hardest part of reviewing can be to remember that you are reviewing not just for yourself but for a large audience that might have different tastes and opinions. You need to take those tastes and opinions into account while expressing your own reasoned account of a book.

How can reviewers remain fair when writing a negative review?

It's important to take into account what kind of book you're re-viewing. The genre often dictates the grounds for judgment. For in-stance, you can't slam a five-volume reference work on health insur-ance for lacking nuance and atmosphere—you look at its breadth of coverage, accuracy, and usefulness. A novel, however, can be assessed by those criteria. The most important thing in a negative review is to back up any criticism with solid evidence, which is why negative re-views can tend to run longer. Also, tone is important: gratuitously nasty reviews call attention more to themselves than to the book, and readers tend not to trust them.

Is there anything else you would like potential reviewers to know about the LJ review process?

I would simply advise them to read *LJ* so they have an understand-ing of our audience, goals, and tone. Libraries must select materials for a broad spectrum of readers, so I would also stress the importance of being objective. Lastly, reviewers should know that while it is not *LJ*'s policy to rewrite reviews, in some cases we must rearrange sentences and clarify points. We strive to preserve the reviewer's opinion.

Heather McCormack is assistant managing editor, *Library Journal* Book Review.

Information Today

What factors should authors consider when choosing a potential publisher for their book?

First and foremost—and this is important for virtually every author—is the focus of the publisher's publishing program. You want a publishing partner that has a track record with your topic (or something close, at least) and knows how to reach the readership. This might seem rather obvious, but if I had a nickel for every hopeful children's book author who approached me over the years (without considering the fact that I have never, ever published a children's book) I wouldn't be worrying about my 401K plan today.

Seriously, it is essential to target your work to publishers who understand the material and the market. Not only is this important to the ultimate commercial success of your book, but a really good fit is your best chance of catching the attention of an editor.

For niche-topic books, including those in the library and information science field, periodicals serving the intended readership are going to be an important means of getting the word out. A publisher that has demonstrated its ability to get its books reviewed and mentioned in professional journals, and its willingness to advertise in and utilize the mailing lists of those journals, must be considered a promising candidate. Information Today, Inc. (ITI) reaches thousands of librarians and information professionals each month through its journals, newsletters, directories, 'zines, Web sites, and conferences—a tremendous marketing advantage for ITI's books. There is another significant benefit of working with a publisher that has multiple product lines: in tough economic times (like these) a diversified company is less likely to scale back or discontinue any one of its activities due to lackluster performance than is a less-diversified firm. When book sales suffer as a result of economic trends and conditions (including library budget cuts), or due to increased competition, the financial pressures on a publisher that relies solely on book sales can be devastating. This is true of both large and small publishers, so be aware and try to choose a publisher with legs.

Of course, identifying appropriate publishers is just the first challenge—making contact that leads to a fruitful two-way exchange is even tougher. If you don't have an agent (and, ironically, an agent can be harder to land than a publisher) you can pretty much forget about the major trade publishers—unless yours is a household name, of course. Small to medium-sized publishers are generally receptive to unagented submissions.

When it comes to the debate over which is preferable—small publisher or large publisher—you will want to keep in mind that I've always edited books for modestly sized publishers, and owned and operated small publishing companies. I'm definitely biased.

In addition to being approachable, small publishers fill important niches that are ignored and misunderstood by the big publishers. And there is the fish-in-a-pond issue; personally, I like small ponds and I think many authors feel the same way. When you are more important to a publisher it inevitably means you will have a greater involvement in the publishing process, a closer working relationship with the decision makers, and an easier time getting information about sales, marketing, distribution, whatever. With a large publisher—as with most types of firms—many if not most decisions are made by committee, and analyzed to death by various departments. This can be frustrating for an author, particularly when her editor or another key contact person leaves suddenly in the middle of the process. I've heard many complaints about books (and authors) suffering as a result of a change in editorial command; this can happen at any publishing house, regardless of size, but the anecdotal evidence I'm aware of suggests there is greater turnover in the editorial departments of large publishers than in those of small ones.

There is another factor worth considering, especially for authors with an interest in writing many books on a particular subject: arguably, a small, independent publishing house is more likely to stick with an author simply because the editor or publisher believes in her than a large firm, which—with a corps of MBAs working behind the scenes if not holding the wheel—will tend to be bottom-line oriented in the extreme. In my experience, only a small percentage of writers write a number of books for one major publisher, but many writers manage a successful long-term relationship (and numerous books) with smaller publishers.

Now, I have to say something nice about big publishers because, after all, they exist and do quite well for their stockholders (however, at this writing Vivendi seems pretty eager to unload Houghton Mifflin). Large publishers have marketing and distribution resources that small publishers can't match, and with their larger personnel resources they can take a project from manuscript to finished book more quickly than a small publisher will. These factors should not be overlooked.

Money isn't everything, and in a niche publishing area you may never get filthy rich (or even plain rich), but I would be remiss if I did not mention the issue of contract terms. The boilerplate differs from firm to firm and you want to be sure you are getting a fair deal—the best possible deal you can. (More on this later.)

It really comes down to your comfort level with the publisher and editor with whom you find yourself dealing. Ask her questions about the process, and see if you share a vision for the book (does she "get it"?). If royalty earnings are important to you, ask for a rough estimate of sales and royalties (and realize it *is* only a rough estimate) based on her experience with similar books. Is it likely you will earn out your advance? How long might that take? If your editor is communicative, patient, and helpful, and if you can establish a positive rapport from the outset, this is a most promising sign. If the editor you are dealing with prior to signing a contract is not responsive, does not return your calls or e-mail messages, and doesn't share your enthusiasm for the project, run, don't walk, to the nearest competitor and see if they can do any better.

Talk to other authors in your field about their publishers. It's not foolproof, but if they are happy, there's a good chance you would be, too. The reverse is also true.

What do you look for in an effective book proposal? What mistakes do authors commonly make when submitting their proposals to Information Today?

It's impossible to overstress the importance of a well-crafted book proposal. If you are famous, or the acknowledged leader in your field, you may be able to get a contract without one, or with something slapdash, but for most writers it's the key to convincing a publisher that you have something important to say and will be able to say it well. Great ideas happen all the time: everyone has them, and I love to hear them, but if the individual with the idea can't or won't follow up with a written proposal there's no way a book is going to result. My file drawers and backup disks are crammed with records of great book ideas that never went anywhere because those who had them did not take the next step and create a proposal.

Beyond the primary purpose of the proposal—which is to present a book's concept and make a case for its publication—it is the most important tool I have for weeding out the semi-serious from the driven individuals, and the good writers from the bad. Semi-serious writers never take the time to develop a really strong proposal, and bad writers are always betrayed by the execution.

Bad grammar, awkward construction, redundancies, spelling errors, and typos in a proposal tell me that the individual is probably unaware of his weaknesses as a writer—if he were not, why would he send it to me like this? This shows poor judgment. A smart writer will always ask a trusted friend or associate to look over his proposal before submitting it. Smart writers are what I'm looking for.

So, it's understating the case to say that carelessness in the preparation of a proposal is a red flag: a poorly executed proposal suggests (or screams) that we will end up with a poorly executed manuscript. Does a great manuscript always result from a great proposal? Not always, but it's a pretty good bet.

Our book proposal guidelines ask potential authors to include or address the following eight items:

1. Suggested title and subtitle
2. Synopsis/overview
3. Preliminary table of contents
4. Graphics
5. Readership
6. Competition
7. Author background
8. Timing on manuscript delivery

How can authors help you market and sell their books? What type of marketing support do you provide them?

Beyond the author's experience, reputation, and ability to explain her topic, we always look for enthusiasm in respect to the marketing of her book. I hope it doesn't sound clichéd, and I certainly don't want to take anything away from the mighty effort that goes into writing a book and then editing and designing it (this is a lot of work), but I like to say "the real work starts once a book is published."

What point is there in publishing a book if the people who might find it useful never hear about it? The answer is, there is none. So, we have to market our books effectively and I believe that the author as ally in this endeavor is a critical factor for most titles. For many years I have studied sales reports and reflected on how sales might be affected by the authors' involvement in promoting the books. While this is an informal survey, to say the least, the impact is clear to me. An author who networks, speaks at conferences, contributes articles to professional journals, and takes part in book signings and media interviews inevitably makes a significant contribution to the sales success of her book. Of course, she needs to get in the habit of mentioning the book when an opportunity presents itself. Some authors are, understandably, a bit nervous about this at first—perhaps worried about being seen as opportunistic—but when an author realizes that most people expect and even want him to talk about his book it starts to become easier.

Let's face it: not everyone is comfortable with public speaking. Some authors are born promoters who will stop at nothing to spread the word about a new book, but many writers are shy by nature and will approach the promotional aspects with some trepidation. We ask and expect our authors to do what they feel comfortable doing to promote their work, and mainly to deliver on any promises they make: if a writer states in his proposal or elsewhere prior to contract signing that he intends to go in front of the public, and to aggressively promote his book, then we may invest in some appropriate publicity and we will expect him to live up to this commitment.

ITI has a marketing department and a full-time book marketing co-ordinator, and we are prepared to support the marketing of each book in a manner that is appropriate given its scope and readership. Some books require a very creative and aggressive marketing effort—this is especially true of those that do not appeal directly to any of ITI's core readership segments (we do occasionally take such books on). Because most of our books do appeal to one or more of our magazine readerships and to our conference attendees and Web site visitors, a key focus of our book marketing effort is to effectively exploit these "captive markets" through house advertising, on-site events at conferences, and direct mail.

I'd advise every author to look for a publisher that wants her to be involved in the marketing of her book and that will support her efforts with an appropriate level of publicity. That describes our operation. Our marketing department gets particularly high marks from me for its interest in working with authors to promote books. To get things rolling we ask every author to complete a marketing questionnaire. This is a fairly extensive list of questions designed to draw as many good ideas out of the author as possible. We even ask them to give us their version of catalog or marketing copy for their book—often the result is very good copy, and at the very least this brings forward ideas that help us develop better copy than we could have otherwise.

Other questions/aspects of the marketing questionnaire include:

- What is unique about the book?
- What newsworthy angles might we cover in the press release?
- What are the primary readerships for the book? Any strong secondary readerships?
- What if any aspects of the book do you consider the strongest feature for broad consumer use?
- In what section(s) of a bookstore would you suggest featuring your book?
- Tell us about any bookstores that might be interested in inviting you to take part in a book signing.
- Is there any potential for your book to be used as a textbook? How and where?
- Suggest professional associations, societies, and publications whose lists might be used in the direct mail marketing of your book.
- Suggest places to advertise your book.
- Suggest potential reviewers of your book (magazines, newsletters, Web sites, radio/TV shows, etc.).
- Suggest news syndicates, newspapers, newsletters, journals, Web sites, etc., that might have an interest in announcing the publication of your book.
- If you would like us to send a news release to your local newspaper, staff publication, alumni journal, etc., please list them.
- Are there any organizations (corporations, online services, etc.) that might be interested in your book for training programs or as a premium?
- Suggest some known experts in the subject area of your book whom we might approach for endorsements to use in cover and promotional copy.

Our marketing department makes a concerted effort to alert the industry press and other media outlets about our books. A press release is produced for every new book and distributed to a growing and well-maintained list of press contacts. With increasing frequency in recent years, the marketing department has been employing professional book publicists to develop publicity campaigns for certain books. This is expensive, and it's not effective or necessary for every book, but when we have a hot topic, a book we feel really good about, and an author who's ready to meet the press we like this investment.

I am a huge believer in the importance of book reviews—some people might say to a fault because I send out many more free review copies in the average month than we see reviews in a year. Still, I make no excuses: you never know when or where that dream review might be published. Furthermore, I believe in a cumulative effect whereby reviewers take us more seriously as they increasingly recognize our commitment to book publishing and our high editorial standards. They need to see our books for this to happen. We send out both pre-pub and on-pub review copies of books, as warranted. I manage the reviewer list personally: I review it for each forthcoming book and handpick the reviewers and experts whose good words can boost sales. This list includes all the important English-language reviewers (and a handful of non-English reviewers) in the field of library and information science as well as business/technology/Internet book reviewers generally, and it is always growing. These days, on average, we mail 75-150 review copies of each book, and we encourage authors to provide us with names and addresses of reviewers we may not know about.

There's a lot more that could be said about marketing—it's definitely one of the parts of my job that is most likely to keep me awake at night. But I love the challenge.

What should authors look for in a contract from a publisher? Are there specific areas in which you or other presses are more open to negotiation than others?

Some publishers (like ITI) offer an advance on royalties, some don't. Some don't offer royalties at all, but instead offer a significant work-for-hire fee. Some report sales annually, while others report semi-annually (like ITI) or even monthly. None of these approaches is intrinsically bad or good—it's really what's important to you, the author, that counts. Clearly, though, if you haven't had previous experience with book publishing agreements you may have difficulty determining what is reasonable and where you can do better: ask someone with a few book contracts under her belt to look at what the publisher sends you; if you can afford it, an attorney *with book publishing contract experience* (emphasis critical) is a great idea.

While it is extremely unlikely you will get everything your lawyer or the Author's Guild recommends, it doesn't hurt to ask the publisher for anything that you feel is important. A publisher that really wants your book will show flexibility in the contract negotiations, and here's something you can bet on: if you read a contract carefully and ask for clarifications and adjustments in an informed, nonconfrontational manner your publisher will respect you all the more for it. This doesn't mean they are going to give in on everything, but where a clause is firm they should at least explain why that is.

Could you talk a little bit about the publishing process and the average time frame of major steps in the process? What should a new author expect after the contract is signed?

The entire process from receipt of an acceptable manuscript to having printed books shipping from the printer can take anywhere from five months to a year (and occasionally longer). For most books, seven to eight months is a good rule of thumb, but of course there are many, many contributing factors.

The process typically goes like this:

1. From our initial conversation with the author about the book, it takes 30-45 days to reach agreement on the details and sign a contract.

2. Authors usually want six to nine months (sometimes a little less and sometimes a little more) to complete the writing and deliver a manuscript to us. Once the manuscript has been delivered:

3. We (the managing editor and/or myself) will usually take 30-45 days to evaluate the manuscript, decide what if any revisions are necessary, communicate any questions or concerns to the author, and officially accept the manuscript for publication. If revisions will be significant we may not accept the manuscript until the author has completed them to our satisfaction.

4. The author will usually answer any queries within a week or two; revisions may take longer (a 30- to 60-day turnaround is not uncommon, depending on the extent of the revision). Once we are satisfied that the manuscript lives up to the promise of the original proposal, and meets our submission guidelines, we assign a copyeditor to work on it.

5. At this point, if not sooner, the author will begin working on a questionnaire designed to help us in planning the catalog listings,

marketing, and distribution of the book. I write the cover and marketing copy for just about every book, but I always start by trying to coax something out of the author (many of them turn out to be better copy writers than they would have thought). By now, we are also thinking of experts for cover quotes, and figuring out how we are going to get a foot in the door with them. Endorsements sell books.

6. Copyediting is typically a one- to two-week process. Once completed:

7. The managing editor creates a production schedule, and the manuscript is moved to the production department for layout. Unless the book is part of a series, or where the layout is to be based on a previously published title, we ask our designer to create sample pages for approval, including the front matter (including the table of contents) and a representative chapter (which will include samples of all fonts, headings, and graphics that will appear in the book). In most cases we approve the design within a few days and the designer gets down to the work of laying out the book.

8. Depending on what else is in the pipeline and the priority assigned to a given book, the complete initial layout can take anywhere from a week to a month, sometimes longer. We refer to the designed pages as a "galley," and this galley inevitably goes back and forth between our editorial and production departments numerous times for corrections before we feel it is ready for the author to review (if all goes well, this back-and-forth process takes no more than two or three weeks).

9. The author receives his galley and is given one to two weeks to review and return it—a little longer if it is a particularly long or complex book. We ask the author to read it very carefully because this is his last opportunity to tweak it (we do not expect revisions at this stage, though sometimes events warrant them). We also ask the author to check every referenced Internet resource at this point to ensure the content and URLs are still valid.

10. By this time we are usually well along with our planned cover design and have either announced publication in our catalog or are preparing to do so (this varies depending on the timing of the book in relation to the production of our semiannual catalog and other

marketing materials). Some authors express a keen interest in the cover design; in such cases we show them a draft early on and encourage feedback. We have an extremely talented group of designers here, and I'm happy to say that our authors are generally delighted with the covers they come up with—I cannot remember a single disappointment in the five-plus years I've been here.

11. Once the author returns the galley, our designer incorporates any necessary corrections or revisions. This usually takes about a week, again depending on the priority assigned to the project and the status of our pipeline.

12. Next the manuscript is turned over to a freelance proofreader. This process usually takes a week or two including shipping time, proofreading, a check and approval of corrections by the managing editor, and the time it takes for our designer to incorporate the corrections.

13. The managing editor and I take a good look at the galley again now to be sure it is ready to be indexed (naturally, it's not a good idea to index a book until the pagination is final). Then, it's on to a professional indexer. The actual indexing and the time to lay out and proofread the index is about a two-week process—sometimes a little longer if there's a lot going on or it's a particularly challenging indexing assignment.

14. While indexing is underway, our production department is getting quotes from the various printers we work with. We look for a combination of things in making the decision on printer: price, quality, and turnaround are all important and need to be weighed. We get quotes from three to five printers for every book.

15. It should be a hop, skip, and a jump to the printer now: we design back ads for the book, check the cover art (and make the necessary spine adjustment), and then I do a final flip of the complete galley. Once the materials ship to the printer, it will be five to eight weeks before printed copies of the book arrive in our warehouse; in the meantime, we see and review blueline proofs of the text, a match print of the cover, and the F&Gs (folds & gathers—the actual printed sixteen-page signatures that, once approved, will be bound inside the book's cover).

Making a book in fifteen easy steps . . . makes me tired just thinking about it!

*How many copies does Information Today sell of an average book in
the library field? How is the final purchase price determined, and what
can authors generally expect in the way of royalties? Is this typical of
library publishing?*

We usually hope and expect to sell at least one thousand copies of
a book, but there are cases where we know in advance that the readership is likely to be in the hundreds. Where the unit sale is going to be
small, the cover price must be high enough to give us some margin.
Some of our books have sold in excess of twenty thousand copies, and
there are usually several published each year that will go on to sell between five thousand and ten thousand copies—most of our books are
on information technology and research topics, so librarians are a primary readership, but to reach these kinds of numbers we have to tap
into some end user markets as well. My experience has been that with a
strong sale to library schools as well as to information professionals a
library-oriented title can expect to sell in the two thousand to three
thousand copy range; if it sells more than that it is probably finding
some additional responsive readerships.

Ah, the mysteries of book pricing! There is a magic formula that
only publishers know—didn't you know that? Seriously, it is a combination of knowing what the market will bear based on past sales of
similar titles (and those of other publishers) and some calculating to
make sure that after expenses and author royalties there's a good
chance you'll have something to plow back into the program. Printing,
paper, and binding (PPB) forms a large part of the cost of producing a
book—though this expense is easily matched or exceeded by editorial,
production, marketing, shipping, and fulfillment costs (marketing expenses alone will often exceed PPB). One formula we do pay attention
to in establishing a minimum cover price is 6X PPB. In other words,
the cover price of a book that costs $4.00 to print should be no less than
$24.00.

I'm going to sidestep the question of potential royalty earnings because this varies so widely depending on number of copies sold, how
they are sold (direct or via the book trade), cover price, and the author's
royalty percentage. I like to avoid creating unreasonable expectations in
regard to author earnings, and since every book is different it would be
hazardous for me to generalize here. However, in my pre-contract
discussions with an author I am always happy to give her an estimate of

likely earnings based on what we know about the book, its readership, and sales of similar titles.

How many books does Information Today publish in an average year? Of these, approximately what percent are directly solicited by editors and what percent are the result of unsolicited queries from authors?

We have increased our output from eight new titles in 1998, the year I joined the company, to about twenty titles annually today. This includes titles in five imprints: CyberAge Books, ITI Books, Plexus Books, ASI Books, and ASIST Monographs. About half of the books begin as unsolicited proposals or query letters, and the rest are by authors we've been chasing after. With the number of magazines we publish, and the conferences we sponsor, I am in the enviable position of having a great many talented writers and editors who are also experienced info pros on my radar screen at any given time. We try to make sure our book program is on theirs, as well.

Is there anything else it would be helpful for new authors to know before embarking on the book publishing process?

We talked earlier about some of the things authors should keep in mind when considering suitable publishers. Here, I will mention some techniques for identifying the right companies.

Some research into titles and topics should be part of your presubmission effort: keyword searching on the major bookseller sites (and in some cases on major search engines) can be tremendously useful. If your book is potentially of broad interest and should be carried in bookstores, I always recommend bookstore browsing as a means of identifying publishers. This will not only help you identify likely suspects but will let you gauge their production values firsthand. And, of course, the fact that the book is in the store in the first place is reassuring. (Tip: when you find a complementary book on the shelf, look to the acknowledgments page and elsewhere in the front matter for mention of the book's editor—if she enjoyed working on this one, and it sold well and made her look good, she might be willing to give you a listen.)

A library with a good, current collection of books in your subject area is another great place to start; a further benefit of being in the library is that the latest edition of *Literary Marketplace (LMP)* is likely to be on the shelf. This directory, published by ITI, provides contact information for U.S. and Canadian publishers (see *ILMP* for international contact info) including names of acquisition editors and their addresses, and can also help confirm a publisher's interest in the type of book you are writing. Publishers are indexed in *LMP* four ways: alphabetically by company name, by geographical location, by type of publication, and by subject matter covered. An invaluable resource for authors, *LMP* is widely regarded as "The Bible of the Book Trade."

I support the idea of multiple submissions. In consumer trade publishing sending a query or proposal to more than one publisher at a time is often frowned upon, but in niche publishing areas like library and information science I think an author should cast the widest net possible. Given that it can take three months or more to get a contract from first approach, this can help ensure the author's topic doesn't lose its currency during the submission phase.

My final words of advice are these: study and practice the craft of writing, "do the pages," seek feedback from friends and peers (join a writers' group if you think you might benefit from regular criticism and support), believe in yourself, be persistent, and don't let rejection by publishers stop you from pursuing your goal. Great writers are made, not born, and motivation and discipline are the most important ingredients for success.

John B. Bryans is editor-in-chief, Information Today Books.

portal: Libraries and the Academy

Could you talk a little bit about the type of articles that appear in portal, *and their length, format, and style?*

portal explores how technology is affecting librarianship and scholarship, as well as the role of libraries in meeting institutional missions. The information revolution presents numerous challenges to librarians, faculty, and administrators in areas including archiving, copyright, and technology-enhanced learning. *portal* covers these and other topics as they relate to the rapidly changing needs of academics and the roles of libraries and librarians. Continuing features address technological issues; research; standards; policy and strategic planning; and reviews of books, databases, and other resources of interest in librarianship and higher education. Article manuscripts are typically twenty pages double-spaced, but are acceptable half as long, twice as long, or longer (article may be divided between two issues). We are interested in highly readable, well-researched, thought-provoking articles that relate specific observations or experiences to broader issues, discuss and disseminate vanguard work, or raise questions and prepare the way for continued research on problems facing librarians and the academy today.

What advantages accrue to authors who submit their work to portal? *Where do these differ from other major journals in the field?*

portal is a peer-reviewed journal, which is always an advantage to authors. More importantly, *portal* has an active mentoring program. This program allows authors to receive help with the creation of the article, rather than writing an entire article only to have it rejected. Some other library associations have mentoring committees, but as far as we know, *portal* is the only journal with a formal mentoring program open to all who apply for help.

portal continues to have a quick time to publication. Articles are refereed in four to six weeks and are often published in the next issue or in the one following. Many other journals have as much as a one-year waiting period for publication.

portal is available electronically via Project MUSE, and the readership through MUSE is much higher than projected readership in the paper environment. In our first year (as of the end of December 2001), we had only 168 institutional subscriptions but there had been nearly 32,000 *portal* article downloads from MUSE. This is relevant for authors who want to be read.

Can you tell me about the history of portal, *and the reasons for which it was founded? How has the journal progressed since its inception?*

portal was founded when Reed Elsevier purchased the *Journal of Academic Librarianship*. The editor and almost a dozen of the referees and column editors did not want to contribute their intellectual talents to Elsevier's bottom line because Elsevier's profit taking and pricing practices have harmed academic libraries so severely. This cadre of experienced journal producers left *JAL* and with the help of the Johns Hopkins University Press were able to found *portal*. We were delighted to be able to distribute *portal* electronically through MUSE, a moderately priced electronic resource.

How does the review process work at portal? *Are all reviewers part of your editorial board, or are manuscripts also sent out to independent reviewers?*

Most reviewing currently is done by members of the editorial board. However, other independent reviewers are employed to help out in special cases.

Please explain your journal's mentoring system: where do you find mentors; what is their involvement in the process; and what benefits have you seen for authors?

The *portal* board and editors are committed to help authors from the moment they decide to engage in research to the moment when they elect to submit the finished product either to *portal* or to some other journal. We foster a supportive and confidential environment for authors in general, but our mentoring program specifically helps them through the rough spots. *portal* mentors are experienced authors and all have volunteered, including members of the Library Research Round Table, members of the editorial board and others. Mentors consult with authors about topic identification and selection, about issues around statistical sampling and survey design, and about crafting the article itself. We believe that early intervention enables aspiring authors to complete strong projects that are likely to be accepted for publication by an independent set of referees. Six mentored articles have been accepted or published to date, and fourteen authors currently are being assisted by mentors.

Do you ever actively solicit contributors to the journal, or does most content originate from unsolicited manuscripts/queries?

We solicit colleagues whom we know to be doing excellent and interesting research and projects, but we also rely on over-the-transom submissions. Our mentoring project brings in additional high-quality submissions.

portal *is electronically archived and available through Project MUSE. Could you briefly explain Project MUSE and what this means for authors? In what other ways has the electronic environment impacted the publishing environment at* portal?

Project MUSE was launched in 1995 to offer the full text of Johns Hopkins University Press scholarly journals on the Web. In 1999, MUSE expanded to become a partnership of nonprofit publishers. From the beginning, MUSE been hailed for its library-friendly policies, reasonable pricing, and user-friendly searching and navigation. Being part of MUSE has energized both the board and authors. Together with the short backlog, timely electronic publication and access are big bonuses to authors and help make publishing in *portal*/MUSE a positive experience. We also handle virtually all of our correspondence by e-mail, from receiving manuscripts to distributing final page proofs to authors as .pdf files.

What advice would you have for writers new to writing for academic journals? What mistakes do you most often see?

The advice I have been giving over my last twelve years as an editor is to get help with the article in its formative stages. Don't let the article be rejected for poor writing, poor statistics, poor idea formation, or sloppy organizational skills. Use the network on your campus to help you avoid these common pitfalls. Use the statistics help desk, the writing laboratory, and all the friends who were English majors. Make the article as good as possible before submission for review by referees.

Another frequent difficulty is not writing an article that can be generalized to the universe of academic libraries. Librarians learn from hearing about projects done in other libraries, but the librarians who write those up need to explain to the audience how their successful project can be successful and should be successful in other libraries.

Finally, ironically: *portal* copy editor Dr. Martha Bright complains regularly about how poorly librarians follow their own rules for citations. Dr. Bright notes that librarian practices are so sloppy that if these articles were handed in as term papers, the librarians could be charged with plagiarism. And, when she asks the librarians to find these citations, they are recalcitrant. Libraries are part of a system that relies on giving credit for intellectual ideas, and it is shameful to think that librarians can't be best practitioners in this area.

*Your contributor guidelines note that "*portal *provides an unbiased outlet for issues that scholars have been unable or unwilling to address in other venues." Can you provide some examples of these?*

We are just getting ready to publish an article that is pretty critical of the big science publishers and their practices. Our editorials, written by Dr. Martin, Dr. Lowry, and me, are frank about the economic problems facing libraries and our continuing difficulties in surviving in this environment.

Approximately what percentage of manuscripts submitted to portal are accepted?

About 76 percent of the submitted manuscripts are published.

Gloriana St. Clair is managing editor, *portal: Libraries and the Academy.*

Information Technology and Libraries

Could you talk a little bit about the type of articles that appear in Information Technology and Libraries, *and their length, format, and style?*

We publish three types of articles: features, communications, and tutorials. Features are generally, although not always, full-blown scholarly research articles, with all that implies, such as literature review, formal footnoting, etc. They are generally longer than a communication, however there is no set length requirement. A communication doesn't usually contain "research" but might still have footnotes. It will more often than not relate how a library solved a particular problem with some kind of technology approach. Tutorials are just what the word suggests: a piece that explains how to use a certain technology to accomplish a certain goal.

Do you ever actively solicit individual contributors to the journal, or does most content originate from unsolicited manuscripts/queries?

Most content originates from unsolicited manuscripts sent to the editor by authors who wish to have their manuscript considered for publication. We do on occasion actively solicit individual contributions. Most often, this happens when a guest editor is putting together a group of writers for a "theme" issue on a particular topic.

ITAL tends to place calls for contributors on relevant e-mail discussion lists for librarians. Do you post such calls elsewhere, or do you receive sufficient response to electronic requests?

So far, we have not posted a call for contributors on a nonlibrary discussion list, however it might be a good idea for us to consider doing that. I would like to increase the number of submissions, and this could help to do so.

How else does ITAL take advantage of the Internet, and how does the electronic environment affect your authors?

I send manuscripts to reviewers via FedEx, but otherwise all correspondence between me and reviewers, board members, and as much as possible, authors (not all authors give me e-mail addresses, however that is a rare exception) takes place via Internet e-mail. My correspondence with ALA Production Services, the group that takes care of the copyediting and page layout of the journal, is also done via e-mail. I send all manuscripts to them in electronic form as e-mail attachments. Proofs are likewise distributed via e-mail as PDF files.

Authors use the electronic environment extensively. Given the technological orientation of *ITAL*, there is almost always some electronic aspect to their articles, which often include screen shots and URLs. Footnotes in particular more often than not these days include a URL and a "last accessed" date. When the final revision of an article is ready to go, it almost always comes via e-mail and almost nobody sends diskettes anymore.

Could you explain the publication process and timeline at ITAL? What should authors expect after turning in a manuscript?

There are always exceptions, of course, but in general here is what happens. When I receive a manuscript, I give it a cursory examination to see whether there is an obvious reason to reject it, e.g., it is clearly out of the scope of *ITAL*. Then it goes into the peer-review process, which should only take three to four weeks, but sometimes is longer, especially if I decide I want a second opinion (which doesn't happen very often). Depending upon the reviewer's recommendation (see next question), the manuscript could be accepted or rejected or, most likely, could require some rewriting, in which case there would be some additional time interval. Once we are ready to accept a manuscript, I ask the author to send me an electronic version of the final document.

When I've received the final manuscript, I target it for an upcoming issue. Since *ITAL* is a quarterly publication (March, June, September, December), I send copy to the ALA production staff at three-month intervals, which are roughly three months ahead of the publication date. So, for example, I could be sending copy for the June issue in late February or early March.

The production process involves a period during which the manuscripts are copyedited. Then we contact authors with questions identified by the copy editors in the first pass through. These could be any number of things, such as a reference doesn't look correct, a sentence or paragraph is not clear as to what the author means, is a particular edit acceptable to the author, etc. Our managing editor works with the authors to resolve these questions, then communicates the results back to production services, where they are incorporated into the emerging issue. A second pass always generates a few more questions that also need to be resolved. Sometimes, although rarely, an article needs a third pass before we can declare the issue ready to go to the printer.

Please explain how the review process works at ITAL, and what reviewers examine when looking at a manuscript. Do you employ a regular board of reviewers, or send manuscripts to subject experts as needed? Are all sections of the journal refereed?

We follow a typical double-blind review process, meaning that the author doesn't know who reviews the manuscript and the reviewer doesn't know who wrote it.

Reviewers are asked to consider several things as they assess a manuscript's potential for publication: Is the topic within the scope of *ITAL*? Is it meaningful and relevant to *ITAL* readers? Does it offer something to the literature? Is it timely? Is it organized well? Does it have a point? Are the citations complete and accurate? Does the manuscript accomplish whatever the author set out to do? Is there something more that needs to be done to make it a more solid contribution?

The reviewer makes a recommendation to me, which is one of the following: 1) accept it and publish as is, or with minor editorial changes; 2) it's almost there but requires some rewriting to make it a solid publishable contribution; 3) it shows some potential, but requires major rewriting and should be reviewed again after a revised draft has be submitted; 4) it does not warrant further consideration for *ITAL*. In all but the first instance, the reviewer should provide specific feedback regarding the manuscript's shortcomings. I pass along to the author any feedback or criticism given to me by the reviewer, paraphrasing it as necessary to preserve the anonymity of the reviewer.

The majority of reviews are done by the *ITAL* Editorial Board; that is their primary duty, and I am fortunate to have a board made up of experienced persons with much expertise in many areas of information technology and libraries. It is not uncommon, however, for me to decide that a particular manuscript would best be reviewed by an expert in the field.

The only sections of *ITAL* not refereed are the editorial page and the book review and software review columns.

Approximately what percent of article submissions to ITAL *are accepted? How often are works sent back to the author for further revision, and what is usually entailed in the revision process?*

Of all the manuscripts submitted to *ITAL*, approximately 50-60 percent are ultimately accepted for publication, but probably at least 90 percent of those required further revision by the author. In my four years with ITAL, I don't think more than five or six have been published without revisions of some kind.

The revision process itself is fairly straightforward. If the review has indicated that the manuscript is pretty close to publishable, I'll just tell the author what more we request in the way of a rewrite and ask them to make those revisions and send me the revised manuscript with a cover letter indicating what they did to satisfy the request. Then I verify that indeed they did so, and we're done.

In those cases where the reviewer has indicated a major rewrite is necessary and that the revised manuscript should be reviewed again, I convey that information and any other suggestions to the author. I ask them to indicate to me whether they plan to do that and submit a revised manuscript. Some I never hear from again; others respond in a negative tone. The majority thank me for the suggestions and promise to submit a revised piece based upon the criticism offered. Those persons almost always follow through with a much better manuscript that the one they originally submitted. It may still take one or two subsequent revisions to get it into top-notch shape, but the end result is a much better work.

What advice would you have for writers new to academic authorship? What mistakes do you most often see?

First, read widely in the scholarly literature and get a feel for what constitutes a good article. Especially read widely in the subject areas that appeal most to you and to which you want to contribute. Second, if at all possible, find a mentor who can help you get started, who can critique your manuscripts and give you advice to help make them better. If written English is not your strong suit (and I direct this advice to native speakers of all languages, including English), please, please, PLEASE get someone to help you with the basics of grammar, syntax, and rhetoric.

The mistakes we see most often would include insufficient literature reviews, weak arguments and inadequate evidence to support a conclusion, poor writing, and stopping before the job is quite finished. All of these mistakes can be alleviated to a great extent by a good mentor.

Finally, while not really something I would call a mistake, yet definitely worth mentioning: More and more articles have accompanying graphic images, which is great, yet often leads to a problem. Most often these graphics are screen shots of some kind, and therefore are at a very low resolution, typically 72 dots per inch (dpi). Since *ITAL* is still primarily a print publication, this is way too low for us. We need at least 300 dpi, and 600 dpi is much better. A good portion of my time is spent telling authors that they need to redo their illustrations at a higher resolution.

Is ITAL *open to newer authors, or should they first gain experience at smaller publications?*

ITAL is definitely open to newer authors, as long as they have something worthwhile to say and can write reasonably well. Just as nobody knows you're a dog on the Internet, neither does the reviewer know whether you've published before.

Dan Marmion is editor, *Information Technology and Libraries.*

Free Pint

Could you talk a little about Free Pint, *and what type of writing you look for?*

Free Pint was first published five years ago to promote my information consultancy Willco Limited (http://www.willco.com). It was from reading e-mail newsletters like Jim Daniel's *BizWeb2000* newsletter that I got the idea of producing a twice monthly e-mail publication, containing valuable articles, and reminding people about the services I offer through Willco.

The newsletter began to grow immediately by five hundred subscribers a month, purely by word of mouth. The content has remained as two articles, a book review, set of "Tipples," and other bits and pieces ever since.

It's now growing at eleven hundred new subscribers a month, with 81 percent of new subscribers signing up through word-of-mouth recommendation.

The content has therefore been tremendously important in encouraging people to spread the word about *Free Pint*. It has always been a business-to-business publication, and when new members have signed up we try and find out a bit about them (such as country, occupation, and how they heard about us).

How much and which sections of the newsletter are freelance written?

Contributed sections include:

- Set of five thirty-word "Tipples" at the top, with a twenty-five-word biography sentence about the contributor. This warms readers up with a "quick hit" of practical tips.
- "Tips" article of about one thousand words, with a one hundred-word biography paragraph
- Book review of about eight hundred words, again with the biography
- "Feature" article of up to fifteen hundred words, with the biography

We then pad this out with content from the *Free Pint* team. This includes an editorial, sponsorship and advertising messages from paying advertisers, and "flyers" promoting our other on-site offerings.

The format is the same for each issue and we use the last issue as a template for the next.

Are you open to working with newer authors with little previous writing experience?

We certainly are, but we are careful at the same time. If the author is unknown to us then we always ask for examples of previous writings and a brief description of work experience. You very quickly get an idea of the person's suitability for writing.

It is very important to maintain a high standard with contributed material. We don't pay for articles, offering instead significant publicity to the author (*Free Pint's* circulation is fifty-three thousand). However, this can attract marketing agencies and others who produce "advertorial" which we refuse to run. In five years we have only had to turn away this type of offering no more than ten times.

Do you actually solicit contributions to the newsletter, or do most articles originate from unsolicited queries? Where do you find potential authors?

As well as refusing advertorial, we also have a policy on "unsolicited article submissions." These tend to be articles offered to us, and many other publications, by self-styled "biz marketing gurus."

Since we have an informal review panel, we cite the panel in turning down submissions. That makes it much less of personal rejection, and we are always extremely polite (even for unsolicited article submissions).

We do, however, use a number of methods for soliciting articles ourselves, and accept offers from suitable authors. We solicit in the following ways:

- by closely managing the *Free Pint* Bar discussion forum to identify people to approach
- from other publications in the information arena
- conference proceedings
- word-of-mouth networking
- asking in the newsletter for contributions
- publishing the Author Update

Whenever we solicit, however, we always make it clear from the start that there are guidelines, and what the remuneration will (or won't) be. It is very embarrassing to introduce these things a little way into the conversation.

Could you describe how your Author Update service works?

The *Free Pint Newsletter* itself is a great way to regularly remind our audience that we exist. Therefore, I thought a great way to keep in touch with authors would be through an Author Update.

This is a brief e-mail newsletter, published quarterly. Past contributors are subscribed to it, and anyone else can choose to subscribe on the Web site. It has a circulation of around five hundred people. The mailing contains suggestions for article topics we'd like to run, and books awaiting review in the *Free Pint* office. Again, we ask potential reviewers to get in touch and to tell us a little about themselves before we continue.

The Author Update works very well, and we currently have enough material booked into the newsletter for the next four months.

What advantages does electronic publication in an e-newsletter such as
Free Pint *offer to authors over publication in traditional print outlets?*

There are various benefits for the author, and for the publisher too. Both parties benefit from a shorter lead-time to publication. Topics can therefore be much more up-to-date, and it is possible to include deep-linking URLs since they are much less likely to have changed. On that note, we check all URLs in all submissions to make sure that they work.

Often the author's work will be more widely read since an e-mail publication may have a much larger circulation than a print one. Also, redistribution of an e-mail newsletter is often easier than a print edition, especially where the recipient is in a different location to the person they pass it on to.

From the publisher's point of view, it is also much easier to change the content of the newsletter, right up until minutes before publication. The time then from publication to receipt by the subscriber can be minutes to hours, rather than days to weeks. Bounces are easier to spot and handle, and of course publishing costs are significantly cheaper.

However, print does hold more "weight" with the recipient, since they can physically touch the publication and may be overwhelmed by lots of e-mails. This is why we also do the following:

- encourage people to print out the newsletter
- make the "subject" of the e-mail easy to spot
- produce a choice of versions, including a fully formatted version of the newsletter in Adobe Acrobat format and an on-site notification

What tips would you have for writers interested in contributing to the publication?

Here are some of my tips for potential writers:

1.   Make sure you adhere to word counts and other guidelines such as formatting. It makes a publisher's life difficult if your contribution is too long, or delivered in Word with bold, tabs, curly quotes, indentation, non-ASCII characters, etc., when what they require is simply plain text.

2.   "Lurk" around the newsletter for a while (like you would on an e-mail discussion list) before contributing. You'll then get a good feel for the type of audience, topics that have or haven't been covered, etc.

3.   If the newsletter has an associated online forum then check that out and possibly get involved. We have spotted a number of potential authors at the *Free Pint* Bar, and indeed some employees too.

4.   Make the most of the promotional paragraph at the end of the article. This is a very powerful marketing tool and must not be ignored.

5.   Ensure that the content is pitched at the right level for the audience and is on a relevant topic. There is nothing worse than pitching the article too low (it will be rejected by the publisher for being trivial) or too high-brow (where the readers will simply stop reading the article, and not get to your biography paragraph).

Is there anything else you'd like to share about your publishing process?

It is tremendously important to have a system in place for managing the publishing process. You need to know when your publication dates are, the copy deadlines, what material you have lined up for which issue, and details about authors and their articles. You also need to keep track of who you've solicited material from, and be thinking about the topics you'd like to cover in the future even if you haven't got a particular author lined up.

A lot of this is simply administrative, and so don't think it specifically needs an experienced editor to manage. We have built an in-house database to manage the whole thing, and it works extremely well.

Finally, make the publishing process and subscriber management as automated and simple as possible. If you are being overwhelmed with handling subscribe requests manually then you will feel discouraged to put effort into the content of your publication.

Publishing an e-mail newsletter can produce significant rewards, but it does take a lot of effort and you constantly have to make sure that you are giving your readership what they want to read.

William Hann is the founder and managing editor of *Free Pint* (http://www.freepint.com).

Bibliography

Allen, Moira. *The Writer's Guide to Queries, Pitches & Proposals.* New York: Allworth Press, 2001.

Alley, Brian, and Jennifer Cargill. *Librarian in Search of a Publisher: How to Get Published.* Westport, Conn.: Oryx Press, 1986.

Axtell, James. "Twenty-Five Reasons to Publish." In *The Pleasures of Academe: A Celebration and Defense of Higher Education,* edited by James Axtell. Lincoln, Nebr.: University of Nebraska Press, 1998: 48-68.

Bahr, Alice, ed. *InPrint: Publishing Opportunities for College Librarians.* Chicago: ACRL, 2001. http://acrl.telusys.net/epubs/inprint.html (5 July 2002).

Bailey, Charles. "Scholarly Electronic Publishing Bibliography." Houston: University of Houston Libraries, 1996-2003. http://info.lib.uh.edu/sepb/sepb.html (9 March 2003).

Block, Marylaine. "Web Contributions and Tenure Decisions." *Ex Libris* 159 (November 14, 2002). http://marylaine.com/exlibris/xlib159.html (20 November 2002).

Bradigan, Pamela S., and Carol A. Mularski. "Evaluation of Academic Librarians' Publications for Tenure and Initial Promotion." *The Journal of Academic Librarianship* 22 (September 1996): 360-65.

Busha, Charles H., and Stephen P. Harter, eds. *Research Methods in Librarianship: Techniques and Interpretations.* New York: Academic Press: 1980.

Camerson, Blythe. *How to Sell, Then Write Your Nonfiction Book.* Chicago: Contemporary Books, 2002.

Carpenter, Kenneth E. "The Librarian-Scholar." *Journal of Academic Librarianship* 23, no. 5 (September 1997): 398-401.

Chepsiuk, Ron. "In Pursuit of the Muse: Librarians Who Write." *American Libraries* 22, no. 10 (November 1991): 988-91.

Crawford, Tad. *Business and Legal Forms for Authors and Self-Publishers.* rev. ed. New York: Allworth Press, 1999.

Crawford, Tad, and Tony Lyons. *The Writer's Legal Guide.* 3rd ed. New York: Allworth Press, 2002.

Crawford, Walt. *First Have Something to Say: Writing for the Library Profession.* Chicago: ALA Editions, 2003.

Day, Abby. *How to Get Research Published in Journals.* Hampshire, England: Gower Publishing, 1996.

DeCandido, GraceAnne. "How to Write a Decent Book Review" (June 1998). http://www.well.com/user/ladyhawk/bookrevs.html (12 January 2003).

Di Vecchio, Jerry. "Transforming an Oral Presentation for Publication." *Library Administration & Management* 12, no. 3 (Summer 1998): 138-41.

Dorn, Fred J. *Publishing for Professional Development.* Muncie, Ind.: Accelerated Development, 1985.

Duranceau, Ellen Finnie. "Publishing Opportunities: Getting into Print or Getting Involved." *The Serials Librarian* 23, no. 3-4 (1993): 253-56.

Ebbinghouse, Carol. "Would You Hire You?: Continuing Education for the Information Professional." *Searcher* 10, no. 7 (July/August 2002): 110-15.

Fox, Mary Frank. *Scholarly Writing and Publishing: Issues, Problems, and Solutions.* Boulder, Colo.: Westview Press, 1985.

Germano, William. *Getting It Published: A Guide for Scholars and Anyone Else Serious about Serious Books.* Chicago: University of Chicago Press, 2001.

Giesecke, Joan. "Preparing Research For Publication." *Library Administration & Management* 12, no. 3 (Summer 1998): 134-37.

Glazier, Jack D., and Ronald R. Powell. *Qualitative Research in Information Management.* Englewood, Colo.: Libraries Unlimited, 1992.

Gorman, G. E., and Peter Clayton. *Qualitative Research for the Information Professional: A Practical Handbook.* London: Library Association Publishing: 1997.

Gordon, Rachel Singer, and Sarah L. Nesbeitt. *The Information Professional's Guide to Career Development Online.* Medford, N.J.: Information Today, 2002.

Haas, Leslie, Suzanne Milton, and Aimee Quinn. "Surviving the Publishing Process: A Beginner's Guide." *RQ* 36, no. 2 (Winter 1996): 230-46.

Harnad, Stevan. "Free at Last: The Future of Peer-Reviewed Journals." *D-Lib Magazine* 5, no. 12 (December 1999). http://www.dlib.org/dlib/december99/12harnad.html (16 September 2002).

Hauser, Thomas. "The 'Standard' Book Contract: An Anti-Trust Lawsuit Waiting To Happen." February 3, 2000. http://www.mediachannel.org/views/oped/bookcontract.shtml (3 July 2002).

Henson, Kenneth T. *Writing for Professional Publication: Keys to Academic and Business Success.* Needham Heights, Mass.: Allyn & Bacon, 1999.

Hernon, Peter. "Research in Library and Information Science—Reflections on the Journal Literature." *Journal of Academic Librarianship* 25, no. 4 (July 1999): 262-66.

Info Career Trends 1, no. 2 (1 Nov. 2000). Theme issue on writing for publication. http://www.lisjobs.com/newsletter/archives2000.htm (14 September 2002).

Isaac, Frederick. "Librarian, Scholar, or Author? The Librarian's New Dilemma." *Journal of Academic Librarianship* 9, no. 4 (September 1983): 216-20.

Jackson, Mary E. "Becoming a Published Author: Eight Simple Steps for Librarians." *Library Administration & Management* 11, no. 1 (Winter 1997): 11-14.

Jacsó, Péter. "Librarians as Digital Authors and Publishers." *Computers in Libraries* 21, no. 5 (May 2001): 52-54.

Johnson, Peggy. "Writing for Publication." *Technicalities* 17, no. 2 (February 1997): 9-11.

Kahle, Brewster. "Way Back When." *New Scientist.com*, http://www.newscientist.com/opinion/opinterview.jsp?id=ns23701 (27 November 2002).

Larsen, Michael. *How to Write a Book Proposal.* Cincinnati, Ohio: Writers Digest Books, 1997.

Levinson, Jay Conrad, Rick Frishman, and Michael Larsen. *Guerilla Marketing for Writers: 100 Weapons for Selling Your Work.* Cincinnati, Ohio: Writer's Digest Books, 2001.

Martin, Susan K., and Charles B. Lowry. "Guidelines for Contributors—*portal: Libraries and the Academy.*" 2001-2002. http://

www.press.jhu.edu/press/journals/pla/information/guidelines.html (6 July 2002).

McClure, Charles R., and Peter Hernon, eds. *Library and Information Science Research: Perspectives and Strategies for Improvement.* Norwood, N.J.: Ablex: 1991.

McKiernan, Gerry. "Web-Based Journal Manuscript Management and Peer-Review Software and Systems." *Library Hi-Tech News* 19, no. 7 (August 2002): 31-43.

Milstein, Sarah. "Scholarly Reviews Through the Web." *New York Times,* August 12, 2002. http://www.nytimes.com/2002/08/12/technology/12NECO.html (28 September 2002).

Neely, Teresa Y. "The Impact of Electronic Publications on Promotion and Tenure Decisions." *Leading Ideas* 10 (October 1999). http://www.arl.org/diversity/leading/issue10/tneely.html (14 November 2002).

Nesbeitt, Sarah L., and Rachel Singer Gordon. *The Information Professional's Guide to Career Development Online.* Medford, N.J.: Information Today, 2002.

Pedley, Paul. "Time Management." *The One-Person Library* 18, no. 2 (June 2001): 4-5.

Powell, Ronald R. *Basic Research Methods for Librarians.* 3rd ed. Greenwich, Conn.: Ablex Publishing Corp., 1997.

Rabiner, Susan, and Alfred Fortunato. *Thinking Like Your Editor: How to Write Great Serious Nonfiction—and Get It Published.* New York: W. W. Norton, 2002.

Riggs, Donald. "Losing the Foundation of Understanding." *American Libraries* 25, no. 5 (May 1994): 449.

—. "Research: Value, Methods, and Publishing." *College & Research Libraries* 60, no. 3 (May 1999): 208-9.

Rochester, Maxine K. "Professional Communication Through Journal Articles." *61st IFLA General Conference—Conference Proceedings—August 20-25, 1995.* http://www.ifla.org/IV/ifla61/61-rocm.htm (18 August 2002).

Rubie, Peter. *The Everything Get Published Book.* Holbrook, Mass.: Adams Media Corporation, 2000.

Schroeder, Carol F., and Gloria G. Roberson. *Guide to Publishing Opportunities for Librarians.* Binghamton, N.Y.: Haworth Press, 1995.

Schuman, Patricia Glass, and Charles Harmon. "From Book Idea to Contract." *Library Administration & Management* 11, no. 1 (Winter 1997): 19-25.

Sellen, Betty-Carol, ed. *Librarian/Author: A Practical Guide on How to Get Published.* New York: Neal-Schuman, 1985.

Shontz, Priscilla K. *Jump Start Your Career in Library and Information Science.* Lanham, Md.: Scarecrow Press, 2002.

Siess, Judith A. *Time Management, Planning, and Prioritization for Librarians.* Lanham, Md.: Scarecrow Press, 2002.

Slater, Margaret, ed. *Research Methods in Library and Information Studies.* London: The Library Association, 1990.

Smallwood, Carol. "School Librarian A.K.A. Published Writer." *Book Report* 13, no. 3 (November-December 1994): 13-14.

St. Clair, Gloriana. "Steps toward Writing a Sure Thing." *Library Administration & Management* 11, no. 1 (Winter 1997): 15-18.

Strunk, William Jr., E. B. White, and Roger Angell. *The Elements of Style.* 4th ed. Needham Heights, Mass.: Allyn & Bacon, 2000.

Vaughan, Liwen. *Statistical Methods for the Information Professional: A Practical, Painless Approach to Understanding, Using, and Interpreting Statistics.* Medford, N.J.: Information Today, Inc., 2001.

Watson-Boone, Rebecca. "Academic Librarians As Practitioner-Researchers." *Journal of Academic Librarianship* 26, no. 2 (March 2000): 85-93.

Weller, Ann C. *Editorial Peer Review: Its Strengths and Weaknesses.* Medford, N.J.: Information Today, Inc., 2001.

Wilder, Stanley. "Dr. Litlove: Or How I Learned to Stop Worrying and Love Library Literature." *American Libraries* 24, no. 7 (July-August 1993): 662-63.

Wood, John. *How to Write Attention-Grabbing Query & Cover Letters.* Cincinnati: Writer's Digest Books, 1996.

Index

About the Author

Rachel Singer Gordon is the former head of computer services at the Franklin Park Public Library, Illinois. She is the founder and Webmaster of the library careers site Lisjobs.com, from which she also publishes *Info Career Trends*, a free, bimonthly electronic newsletter on career development issues for librarians. Since 2002, she has been the "Computer Media" review columnist for *Library Journal*. She has written and presented widely on the intersections between technology and librarianship, and her published work includes *Teaching the Internet in Libraries* (ALA Editions, 2001), *The Information Professional's Guide to Career Development Online* (Information Today, 2002), and *The Accidental Systems Librarian* (Information Today, 2003). Rachel holds an MLIS from Dominican University and an MA from Northwestern University.